CERAMIC ART OF THE MALIBU POTTERIES 1926 — 1932

CERAMIC ART OF THE MALIBU POTTERIES
1926 – 1932

BY
Ronald L. Rindge

AND
Thomas W. Doyle
Toni Doyle
Charlotte H. Laubach
Frederick C. May
Judge John J. Merrick
John F. Rindge

EDITED BY
Marcia Page

Published by
THE MALIBU LAGOON MUSEUM
Malibu, California

Distributed by
The University of Washington Press
Seattle and London

DEDICATION

TO THE PEOPLE OF MALIBU POTTERIES whose enterprise, artistic talent, and technical expertise created some of the finest ceramic art the world has ever known for the benefit and enjoyment of future generations.

Published by
THE MALIBU LAGOON MUSEUM
Box 291
23200 Pacific Coast Highway
Malibu, California 90265
213 / 456-1770

Art Director,
    Max King, Amsterdam King Associates
    Santa Monica, California
Photographers,
    Catherine Durlock, Ed Foster, Jane Hemenez,
    Charlotte Laubach, Fred May, Mike McCombs,
    Nancy McFadden, Marc Muench, Andrea Page,
    John Rindge, Ronald Rindge, Sue Rindge,
    Toby Schreiber, Robert Sinclair, Tom Vinetz,
    Wende Wagner, Wayne Wilcox
    – for individual credits, see page 130

Printed in Singapore

First Edition
Second Printing, 1994

ISBN   0-295-97410-9
ISBN   0-295-97372-2 pbk.

fig. 2

fig. 3

PREFACE AND ACKNOWLEDGMENTS

PRIOR TO 1980, INFORMATION ABOUT Malibu Potteries, and its designers and craftspeople, was almost non-existent. However, in the summer of 1980, the Los Angeles Craft and Folk Art Museum, with David Greenberg as guest Curator, sponsored an exhibit on Malibu tile. The Museum published a colorful catalogue, *Malibu Tile,* which contained an informative essay written by Kathryn Smith about Malibu Potteries. Shortly after this exhibit and publication, the mists obscuring the history of Malibu Potteries began to disperse as people who had actually worked there became known to the authors of this book.

Fr. Ronald Colloty, O.F.M., Retreat Master at Serra Retreat in Malibu, met Inez Johnson von Hake, a designer and illustrator who had been employed at Malibu Potteries between 1927 and 1932. Fr. Ronald put Inez in touch with the authors who are members of the Malibu Historical Society and the Malibu Lagoon Museum. Now two former employees were known: salesman Kingsley Sopp and Inez von Hake. Inez provided burgeoning information about Malibu Potteries by promptly introducing the authors to Philip Keeler, son of the late Rufus B. Keeler, the Oper-

ating Manager of the Potteries, and several other former employees including J. Donald and Dorothy Prouty, Lillian Ball, and Margaret Curtis Smith. Shortly after the opening of the Malibu Lagoon Museum in October, 1982, additional former employees were discovered including Glen Dawson, Harry Dellamore, Sarah Estrada Durant, and Eleanor Parker Rorick. James E. Handley, son of the late William Handley, contacted the Museum and provided information about his father's activities at Malibu Potteries. We are especially grateful to Inez von Hake, Philip Keeler, and all those Malibu Potteries alumni or their relatives who contributed so importantly to the content of this book, including donation or loan of many items depicted in this book. We are indebted to the late Glen Dawson, J. Donald Prouty, and Kingsley Sopp who left us the legacy of their memories of Malibu Potteries.

In addition to the above-named contributors, we also acknowledge our gratitude to the following persons or institutions who so graciously gave of their time, provided or assisted in obtaining information, or made available various ceramic products shown in this book. ➤

---

overleaf
fig. 1
Grand staircase, Los Angeles residence. Saracen stair-risers: step 1, E29; step 2, E2; step 3, E36; step 4, E49. Patterns repeat on ascending stairs.

fig. 2
Persian rug panel, 18" x 48" (without border tile), designed by J. Donald Prouty. Saracen panels E622-P1, page 29, SPC. See figs. 3, 151, 152.

fig. 3
P. 29 SPC, Persian rug panel, E622P-1. See figs. 2, 151, 152.

(*acknowledgements continued*)

Sharon Adamson
Harvey Anderson
Edward J. Avila, Commissioner, Board of
    Public Works, City of Los Angeles
Herve Babineau
Robert G. Begley
Michael Braun
Louis T. Busch
California Department of Parks and Recreation
Stephen L. Champlin
Harry and Denise Chandler
Jack Chipman
Fr. Ronald Colloty, O.F.M.
Bro. Antonine Correa, O.F.M.
Rhoda-May Adamson Dallas
Robert De Pietro
Pam Dillingham
Tom Dobyns
Docents of the Malibu Lagoon Museum
George Duncan
Patrick H. Ela, Director, Los Angeles Craft and
    Folk Art Museum
Delleen Enge
Peter and Kathryn Forgie
Franciscans: *Order of Friars Minor* (O.F.M.)
Tina Gale
David Gebhard
Arloa Goldstone
Carol Gordean
Jane Hemenez
Fr. Clifford Herle, O.F.M.
Leonard Hill
Daniel Hoye
Irene Hufford
Dr. and Mrs. Robert Huizenga
Jim Jaffe
Fred Johnson
Debbie King
George and Paula Labrot
Claude and Ellen Lagardére
Peter Laubach
David and Margaret Lederer
Ruthann Lehrer, former Director
    Los Angeles Conservancy
Mrs. William Lochheim
Los Angeles Craft and Folk Art Museum

Paul McCarty, A.I.A., City Architect,
    City of Los Angeles
Bro. Bede McKinnon, O.F.M.
Malibu Historical Society
Marilyn Marble
Julie May
Mayan Theater
Marge Merrick
Mission San Miguel
Mission Santa Barbara
Katherine Moret, Executive Director,
    Project Restore, City of Los Angeles
Henry Morse
Joanne Nelson
James "Bow" O'Barr, Curator,
    Scotty's Castle, Death Valley
Fr. Salvador Parisi, O.F.M.
Oris Payton
Anne Rindge
Sue Rindge
Toby Schreiber
Serra Retreat
Sylvia Rindge Adamson Sheridan
Joseph Smith
St. Francis Retreat, San Juan Bautista
Bob Storms
Jackie Sutton
Joseph A. Taylor
Tile Heritage Foundation
Mrs. E.J. (Billie) Ulrich
Dr. David and Katharine Viscott
Wende Wagner
Carolyn Wallace
Marc Wanamaker
Leon Williams, Office of City Architect,
    City of Los Angeles
Robert Winter

—*With gratitude to all of the above from the authors*—
    Thomas W. Doyle
    Toni Doyle
    Charlotte H. Laubach
    Frederick C. May
    John J. Merrick
    John F. Rindge
    Ronald L. Rindge

TABLE OF CONTENTS

◀ *fig. 4*

fig. 4
*Cuerda seca tile table top, 42"
diameter, see fig. 6. Lobby of
office building, Los Angeles.
See fig. 5, 6.*

fig. 5
*One square foot of fine,
crystalline, crackle overglazed
faience tile in fig. 4.[1] Tile not
listed in Standard Catalogue.*

fig. 6
P. 13 SPC, tile table top.

fig. 6

fig. 5

CERAMIC ART OF THE MALIBU POTTERIES
1 9 2 6 – 1 9 3 2

*STOCK NUMBERS appearing in
this book are taken from the
Malibu Potteries Standard
Catalogue (SC) or from the
Salesmans Pocket Catalogue
(SPC). If the item is listed in the
Standard Catalogue, only the
stock number is given, i.e.
A60, B125, E65. If an item is only
listed in the Salesmans Pocket
Catalogue, the description of the
item is followed by the page
number and the letters, ''SPC,''
i.e. ''42" diameter table top,
p.13 SPC.''*

*THE STOCK NUMBER INDEX in
the back of this book lists in
numeric sequence the Saracen
and Moorish stock numbers
(which were preceded by the
letter ''E'') as printed in the Standard Catalogue.
The index shows stock code, size,
S or M for Saracen or Moorish,
the page number in the Standard
Catalogue, the fiqure number in
this book if the page is reproduced herein, followed by other
figure numbers which pertain to
that particular stock code.*

CERAMICS THE OLDEST OF THE CRAFTS

THE MALIBU POTTERIES produced ceramic art from 1926 to 1932, a brief period in the history of a craft which began thousands of years ago. Rufus B. Keeler, the manager of Malibu Potteries, speaks of that history in his paper presented in the 1920's to a convention of the Tile and Mantel Contractors Association of America. The following excerpts also include background information on the state of the ceramic craft in the United States and California when Malibu Potteries began operations in 1926.

fig. 7
fig. 8

CHAPTER ONE

6

fig. 9

THE OLDEST OF THE CRAFTS
by Rufus B. Keeler

"You tile and mantel contractors have reason to be proud of the fact that you represent the oldest craft known to mankind.

Long before our primitive forefathers had discovered iron, or fire, or water-power; indeed, almost while they were awakening to the possibilities of pieces of stone as instruments of warfare and of utility, they were beginning to fashion strange things of clay. Scientists tell us that the Paleolithic people, who came on the scene between 25,000 and 40,000 years ago, and who probably represent the earliest history of the creature known as Man, worked in clay. They fashioned strange pots and jars and other utensils, and had learned enough to get such handiwork in the sun to dry and harden.

Then in the course of time one of our ancestors learned how to strike fire by rubbing sticks of wood together. Later, his primitive associate of name unknown discovered that clay had a tendency to vitrify when subjected to intense heat, and so the pots and jars were burned in the first rough kilns, and blocks of clay for the walls of huts were hardened and made weather-proof in the same manner.

As the years went on, men learned how to mix the clay with such substances as flint, feldspar and other earth deposits, and finally the use of pigments to give varying colors, and the making of all sorts of figures and designs, gradually developed.

That is merely a brief summing up of the history of the things we now classify under the general term, "Ceramics," and it is therefore the abbreviated history of what we now call Tile.

When I speak of Tile, I refer to a material with which you are all familiar because of its widespread and growing use; a material which you immediately associate with any service where extreme cleanliness

fig. 10

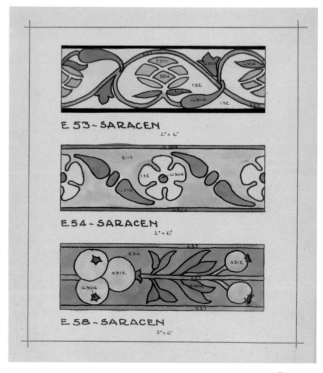

fig. 11

is essential, and which you are all coming to use more and more for decorative purposes in your libraries, hallways, sun-porches, and in public buildings of all kinds.

The decorative possibilities inherent in Tiles were genuinely appreciated in the Middle Ages. Many of the floors laid in that period showed very beautiful effects in the way of pattern and color combinations.

In the south of Europe, many centuries ago, both floor and wall tiles were much used, and this branch of craftsmanship and artistry was later taken up by the Moslem people with striking results in many of the most famous structures of the old world.

In Cairo, Damascus, and other Levantine cities, the art of tile making advanced to such a point that squares containing only a few tiles have been sold for large prices as works of rare value, but even these, fine as they were, did not compare with the tiles of the Persian mosques, where some of the most superb installations in the world are to be found.

The Spanish specialized in Tile several centuries ago, and notably brilliant effects have been wrought there in gold and colored tiles. The appreciation of this material which manifested itself in such splendid structures as the Alhambra and the Granada was transplanted to our own continent, in Mexico, where some of the most magnificent achievements in the use of tiles are to be seen to this day.

The Gothic revival in England between the years 1840 and 1870 brought with it a renewed interest in the tile work of the medieval period, and for years Great Britain led the world in the manufacture of this material, the United States doing considerable importing of tile from England during the time named. Tiles of great refinement and beauty were also made on the continent of Europe, especially in France.

Only a generation or two ago the making of tile began in earnest in the United States. But while it is really an infant enterprise here, in comparison with its age and traditions, it today occupies an important place in our industrial life, and tile last year led all building materials in the percentage of growth of sales over previous years.

The marked difference between our ancestral races and the civilization of today is that whereas the craftsmen and artists of earlier times wrought wonderfully for the beautifying of their temples, mosques and shrines, they did so at the expense of their homes, which were generally sadly neglected. Most of the earlier people had strikingly beautiful places in which to worship, but their homes were crude and, with few exceptions, unattractive.

The modern householder, however, considers his home as of first importance, and the result is that everybody in these days, with the exception of the few who are unable to appreciate or too poor to buy, thinks more or less of those beautifying touches which make the home more than mere shelter.

Beauty and sanitation in the home never before commanded the attention that they do today. This is one of the encouraging proofs that the home itself—the very heart of the ideals and principles which make for a better civilization—is more appreciated as an institution.

Tile meets the advanced requirements of beauty in the modern home for the same reasons that it commanded the admiration of artisans, artists, architects and builders centuries ago. If such a material is beautiful for the cathedral, it is beautiful also for the home, for it is a material of such adaptable service that it can properly be used in the modest structure or the most pretentious.

fig. 12

7

fig. 10
Line drawing from Handbook of Ornament (Meyer, 1957) showing historical influence on Malibu tile design.
Top: Persian, metal vessels, (Racinet). See fig. 11.
Bottom: Intarsia, Sta. Maria in Organo, Verona, 1499. See fig. 11.

fig. 11
Watercolored page, Salesman's Scale Catalogue.
E53 and E58, see fig. 10.

fig. 12
8-point, star-shaped tiles.
Top: Faience tile, 16th c., depicting a ram.
Bottom: Malibu "tea tile" with ram design, patterned after Persian "Stellar" tiles, 13th and 14th c. (Newcomb, 1925, no. 3, p. 23).
For other Malibu "tea tile" designs, see fig. 142.

figs. 13 — 21
Watercolor illustrations by J. Donald Prouty from Architectural Monographs on Tiles and Tilework (Newcomb, No. 5 & 7).

fig. 13
Mural faience from Mosque of Amir Sheykhu, Cairo. Historical influence on Malibu tile designs: E114 and E128.

fig. 14
Faience mosaic from a Medressda (school) at Konia. Historical influence on Malibu tile designs: E107.

fig. 15
Tiled design from the Mirab (prayer-niche), Mosque of Amir Sheykhu, Cairo. Historical influence on Malibu tile designs: E562, E28, E123.

fig. 16
Tile pattern from Mosque of Amir Sheykhu, Cairo. Historical influence on Malibu tile design: E102.

fig. 17
Tile fragment of the Earliest Period, Dome of the Rock, Jerusalem. Historical influence on Malibu tile design: E115.

fig. 18
Tile Fragment, First Period, Dome of the Rock, Jerusalem. Historical influence on Malibu tile designs: E3.

fig. 19
Ceramic frieze from the Dome of the Yechil Turbeh (Green Tomb of Mohammed I), Brusa. Historical influence on Malibu tile designs: E52, E55.

fig. 20
Decorated Tunisian tile. Historical influence on Malibu tile designs: E40, E535.

fig. 21
Decorated Tunisian tile. Historical influence on Malibu tile designs: E610, E532. See also fig. 222.

fig. 13

fig. 14

fig. 15

fig. 16

fig. 17

fig. 18

fig. 19

fig. 20

fig. 21

The first problem in the matter of home decoration is represented by floors. The floor is the decorative foundation of the room. It is the starting point in the ascending scale of color tones, and as such, it should always be darker in color value than the side walls. For the same reason, and in the same degree, the walls should be darker than the ceiling. Never have these three units – the floor, the walls and the ceiling – or any two of them – of the same color or tone value. They must contrast in the order named, if your room is to be proper from the decorative standpoint. We get this correct plan of tone variation from Nature herself.

Nature's floor, the earth, is darkest; her walls, the trees and foliage, and the hills and mountains, the atmosphere about us,

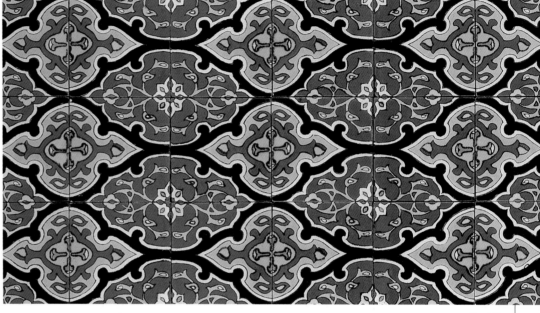

fig. 22

fig. 22
Eighteen tile pattern, E610. See figs. 191, 192, 199.

fig. 23
Decorative plate, 8" diameter, cuenca technique. See fig. 153.

form the next general color tone; and the ceiling is the bright sky of the day, and the night Heavens, studded with stars.

The observance of this simple color formula may be of help to some of you in determining just what your interior decorating scheme shall be. To such a formula, tiles lend themselves admirably, because their range – from the softest natural shades to the brightest, sharpest colors – is unlimited."

Malibu Potteries was founded in response to the strong and growing demand for ceramic tile by architects and builders in the 1920's. Inspired by traditional designs, yet responsive to contemporary themes, the company produced ceramics which remain as outstanding examples of the human need to make the functional also beautiful.

fig. 23

HISTORY OF MALIBU POTTERIES

T HE HISTORY OF MALIBU POTTERIES involves several major factors: the history of the Rindge family and their Malibu Ranch, the architecture and economy of the 1920's and 1930's, and the ceramics wizard who conducted the operations, Rufus B. Keeler. Malibu Potteries was founded in 1926 by May K. Rindge, the widow of Frederick Hastings Rindge, through her Marblehead Land Co. The Rindges were the last owners of the Spanish land grant known today as Malibu.

fig. 24
fig. 25

fig. 26

overleaf
fig. 24
1932 aerial photo showing portion of Malibu Ranch with Malibu Potteries beach location (lower center) and May K. Rindge's un-completed mansion in Malibu Canyon (upper left quadrant).

fig. 25
Twelve tile Saracen pattern, E542.

fig. 26
Ceramic medallion containing the Rindge Coat-of-Arms executed in tile and encased in a Della Robbia-type wreath. The medallion was damaged when it fell to the ground during the 1970 fire at Serra Retreat.

fig. 25

FREDERICK AND MAY RINDGE

Frederick Hastings Rindge first visited California in 1870 as a boy of 13, a passenger on the Union Pacific Railroad's first through train from the East to San Francisco. He would return several times in following years until he brought his bride, Rhoda May Knight, to establish their permanent home in 1887.

Born in Cambridge, Massachusetts, Frederick Rindge was a descendant of a family who migrated to America from England in 1638. As the only surviving child of six siblings, he was educated with particular care, attending Harvard College and also traveling extensively in Europe and the United States. In 1883 he succeeded to his father's estate which was in excess of $2 million.

Rhoda May Knight Rindge (popularly known as May K. Rindge) was born on May 9, 1864 in Trenton, Michigan. She was a teacher when she met Frederick Rindge. They were married on May 17, 1887 and had three children: Samuel Knight Rindge, Frederick Hastings Rindge, Jr., and Rhoda Agatha Rindge.

In 1892, the Rindges purchased the 13,000 acre Rancho Malibu from Henry Workman Keller at a price of $10.00 an acre. With the purchase of Rancho Malibu, Frederick Rindge realized his dream of the ideal country home: "A farm near the ocean, under the lee of the mountains; with a trout brook, wild trees, a lake, good soil, and excellent climate, one not too hot in summer."[1] He built a large ranch house in Malibu Canyon (beneath present-day Serra Retreat) to serve as headquarters for Rancho Malibu. Rindge was a philosopher, poet-writer and man of deep spirituality who loved to ride the reaches of his ranch, dream dreams and make plans. In 1898 he wrote a beautiful book, *Happy Days in Southern California,* in which he recounted his interesting and spiritually sat-

fig. 27
Rindge family portrait, circa 1900. Left to right: May K. Rindge, Rhoda Agatha Rindge, Samuel Knight Rindge, Frederick Hastings Rindge, and Frederick Hastings Rindge, Jr.

isfying experiences of living on the ranch, and in which he envisioned Malibu as an "American Riviera" rivaling the seaside showplaces of Italy and France.

The Rindge family occupied two homes in the Los Angeles area. Their town residence at 2263 Harvard Boulevard still stands today and is designated as an historic-cultural monument by the Los Angeles Cultural Heritage Board. The family visited their Malibu Canyon home on week-ends and during much of the summer season. In 1903 the Malibu home was destroyed by a disastrous brush fire. Following the fire, the family built tent houses and a cabin to house the kitchen and dining room for their Malibu accommodations.

Frederick Rindge died unexpectedly at age 48, on August 29, 1905, at Yreka, California. His widow was left to manage her husband's business affairs and to continue to strive for the dreams they mutually shared for the Malibu Ranch.

fig. 27

THE MALIBU RANCH

Following her husband's death, May Rindge tried to keep the ranch intact by building a railroad in Malibu, and also engaged in a costly seventeen-year legal battle with the State over the land rights to build a public highway through the ranch. In 1921, The Marblehead Land Company (named after Marblehead, Massachusetts, where the Rindge family maintained a summer residence), with Mrs. Rindge as president, became the owner of Malibu.

It was an era of high fences, armed riders to keep out trespassers and surveying parties, and costly and complicated court cases in the State and United States Supreme Courts. Finally, in 1925 the State purchased, through condemnation proceedings, a right-of-way through the Rancho. J. Donald Prouty, hired as designer for Malibu Potteries, recalls the scene when he first came to work:

> When we arrived, she [Mrs. Rindge] or the Marblehead Land Company had already fenced the lost right-of-way on both sides to exclude trespassers from the beach on one side and the foothills on the other. Every other fence post had an enameled sign reading: "Private property, keep out, no picnicking, no stopping, no hunting." Armed riders patrolled the fence night and day . . .² Only those with legitimate business were permitted to drive through.³

The new coastal Roosevelt Highway was completed between Santa Monica and Oxnard and opened to through traffic on June 29, 1929. Another Malibu Potteries employee, Eleanor Rorick, describes her family's reaction to the new road:

> My father used to take us on Sunday drives to the country-side and down the Malibu coast road in our Overland touring car. I think my father must have taken us the very day it was opened to the public. The farther we went up the Malibu, the rougher and more frightening it became. My father was determined to see the forbidden territory.⁴

Mrs. Rindge was determined to carry out her husband's plans to develop an "American Riviera" on the Malibu coast. In 1926 she offered some of the beach frontage, originally for lease, and later for sale. 1926 was also the year she started Malibu Potteries. The Rindges' original plans called for a "Great House" to be built in Malibu Canyon over-looking the sea. In 1929 she started construction of a 50-room house on a site her husband had named "Laudamus Hill." The house was to have three wings, one for each of her three children and their families, but it was never completed. The Malibu Potteries produced large quantities of custom-designed tile for the floors, walls and ceiling decorations. Mrs. Rindge died on February 8, 1941, at the age of 77. In 1942 her unfinished dream house, its 26 acres of land, and thousands of beautiful tiles were sold for $50,000 to the Franciscan Order (Order of Friars Minor) to become the Serra Retreat (see Chapter VIII). On September 25, 1970, the retreat house and most of its unique tile were destroyed by a catastrophic brush fire pushed by the dreaded "Santa Ana" winds described so vividly by Frederick H. Rindge in *Happy Days in Southern California*:

> But now the terrific wind assumes control of the blaze, and, with a sweeping rush, the fire speeds onward in its deadly course. The wind and the fire race as for life . . . the flames do not stop. The death wind has three days to blow, and does not dream of ceasing. To the farmers and the moun-taineers the vibrating air is sounding the death knell of their hopes.⁵

The Franciscans rebuilt much of what was lost and have continued to operate their haven of peace.

THE MALIBU POTTERIES

The founding of Malibu Potteries in 1926 came about partly as a response to the strong demand for decorative ceramic tile used in the prevalent Medi-terranean and Spanish Revival architecture of the 1920's. Also, Mrs. Rindge planned to build structures in that style on the ranch, in keeping with the plans for developing an "American Riviera." Further, it was logical to take advantage of the area's natural re-sources. The ranch had an abundance of good quality red and buff burning clays as well as a plentiful water supply from a spring in nearby Sweetwater Canyon. The opening of the new highway provided good transportation routes to rail and shipping centers in Santa Monica, Los Angeles and San Pedro as well as providing access to a plentiful labor pool in the Santa

fig. 28
Manufacturer's stamp, "Malibu," impressed into clay. Relatively few of the thousands of tiles produced by Malibu Pot-teries were marked, "Malibu," by stamp or by hand inscription.

Monica-Los Angeles area.

The site selected for the Potteries was located about two miles west of Las Flores Canyon and about ½ mile east of Malibu Pier along 1,500 feet of beach frontage. Donald Prouty reports that even then the area was a popular movie location:

During the two years we were at Malibu the only use to which the pier was put was as a point of embarkation for camera launches of movie companies engaged in filming sea epics in vogue at that time, on and around wooden sailing ships anchored off the Malibu shore. The rugged unspoiled coast without structures, chimneys, water tanks and transmission lines, provided a fine background when cameras panned that way. While the filming was in progress, I spent many late afternoons on the beach attempting to paint the magnificent old windjammers.[6]

With the decision made to commence a full-line ceramic tile factory on her Malibu ranch, Mrs. Rindge then had to locate a manager knowledgeable and expert in the ceramic industry to operate the plant. She found Rufus B. Keeler, one of California's foremost ceramists of the era, and retained him to construct and operate Malibu Potteries. It was Keeler who formulated the secret glazes at Malibu Potteries, renowned for their color and clarity.

The popular myth that Mrs. Rindge imported Italian ceramists to build the Malibu Potteries and to work in the plant was refuted by employee Inez von Hake: "It was Rufus Keeler who hired all the employees. No tile makers were brought from any other country."[7]

In 1929, at the start of the Great Depression, production at the plant was closed down for several months. Donald Prouty, one of those employees "temporarily laid off," describes the situation:

It was probably a combination of a slowdown in the con-struction boom, which had started in the 20's, reducing demand for items in full stock and lack of prospective custom orders. The decision to shut down came from Marblehead Land Co.; perhaps they were feeling the financial portents preceeding the actual crash that started the Depression.[8]

During the night hours of November 11-12, 1931, the factory was swept by a fire which raged for seven hours. The November 12, 1931 issue of the *Santa Monica Evening Outlook* stated that the fire originated in the overhead machinery in the clay preparation room at the east end of the plant. The article quotes Rufus Keeler as saying that almost 50 per cent of the building and inventory was destroyed, with the loss estimated to range from $25,000 to $75,000.

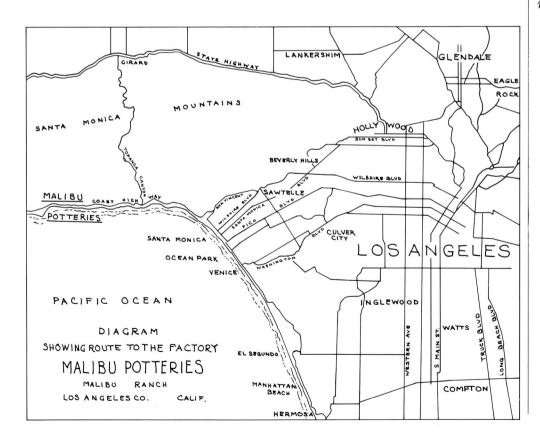

fig. 29
Map of Santa Monica Bay entitled, "Diagram showing route to the factory — Malibu Potteries — Malibu Ranch — Los Angeles, Co. Calif." Note San Fernando Valley community designations: "Girard," now Woodland Hills; "Lankershim," now North Hollywood. Circa 1926.

15

fig. 30

The plant operated partially and sporadically following the fire and was closed again in 1932. It never re-opened due to the effect of the Great Depression coupled with the steep downturn in new construction in the early 1930's. A cryptic article in the January 20, 1940 issue of the *Santa Monica Evening Outlook* announced the final abandonment of the operation:

> *With the machinery and the equipment of the Malibu Potteries being sold for junk by the Marblehead Land Co., Malibu interests indicated today that the tile manufacturing venture has been definitely abandoned by the Rindges.*

During the winter of 1983, a segment of the original office floor was unearthed by stormy seas, 51 years after closing of the plant—a ghostly remnant of the once prosperous Malibu Potteries.

At full capacity production (See Chapter Three), approximately 125 full and part-time people were employed: artists, chemists, engineers, designers, illustrators, salesmen, "claymen," pressers, glazers, draftsmen and administrative personnel. The remainder of this book covers in detail the people, processes and products of Malibu Potteries, under the inspired management of Rufus Keeler.

fig. 30
A dramatic 100-year storm in 1983 unearthed this segment of the original office floor. A piece of this floor is on display at the Malibu Lagoon Museum. The same pattern exists in the first-floor guest bedroom of the Adamson House. See fig. 113.

fig. 31
Newspaper accounts of November 11/12, 1931 fire at Malibu Potteries and abandonment of the venture in 1940, including 1931 photos of burned factory.

Nov. 12, 1931
Santa Monica Evening Outlook
Malibu Pottery Swept by Fire
Industrial Plant Damage Estimated at From $25,000 to $75,000

Though officials today were unable definitely to say what caused the fire that swept through the buildings of the Malibu Potteries Co., on the Roosevelt Highway last night, they announced that new buildings will be started immediately in order to fill thousands of dollars worth of orders on hand.

Insurance men and company heads today viewed the ruins left by the flames which were not brought under control until early this morning by firemen from the forestry stations at Las Flores, Escondido and Topanga canyons.

Jan. 20, 1940
Evening Outlook
Malibu Properties Project is Abandoned

With the machinery and the equipment of the Malibu Potteries being sold for junk by the Marblehead Land Co., Malibu interests indicated today that the tile manufacturing venture has been definitely abandoned by the Rindges.

Art Jones, Malibu real estate operator, reported today that the main building of the plant would either be torn down or remodeled as the owners of the ranch are disposing of all the machinery, equipment and supplies.

fig. 31

RUFUS B. KEELER, MANAGER

The information which follows on Mr. Keeler's life was obtained from his son, Philip Keeler, through interviews or correspondence with people who worked for Mr. Keeler in the 1926-1932 era, through his personal collection of journals, photographs, books and other papers thoughtfully donated to the Malibu Lagoon Museum by Philip Keeler, and from an extensive interview with Philip Keeler by historian Daniel Hoye on June 7, 1986.

The personal qualities of Rufus B. Keeler as expressed by those who worked for him at Malibu Potteries reveal a multi-faceted man. Salesman Kingsley Sopp wrote:

> Mr. Keeler was an outstanding ceramic engineer in developing decorative tiles and the glazes in the many colors required. He was very capable. He had spent years researching Spanish and Moorish decorative tile. The color glazes he had developed were perfect colors of the originals (Spanish—Moorish colors). I believe that he made the most complete and most beautiful line of this type of tile that has ever been made.[9]

Donald Prouty described Mr. Keeler as:

> . . . The Ceramist—he alone formulated all of the glazes. . . . Mr. Keeler was a fine ceramist and a good plant operating manager.[10]

Lillian Ball remembers Keeler as an expert, yet cautious, canoeist who would take several employees on a canoe ride in the ocean at lunch time or after work. He was a strong swimmer. James Handley, who as a boy visited the plant with his father, designer William E. Handley, recalls that it was Mr. Keeler who taught him how to swim. Inez von Hake also remembers lunch hour swims led by Keeler.

The Keeler family immigrated from England between 1630 and 1640 to Norwalk, Connecticut, eventually settling in Ridgefield, Connecticut. Rufus B. Keeler was born in Bellingham, Washington on August 5, 1885 and was reared and educated in San Francisco. In 1905 he started his career in the ceramic industry by joining the Carnegie Brick and Pottery Company in Carnegie, California. Here he met his future wife, Mary, who also worked for the company as a secretary and school teacher. Carnegie produced bricks, flooring, and terra cotta building ornamentation which was used extensively to rebuild San Francisco after the devastating 1906 earthquake. Keeler joined the American Ceramic Society in 1909.

Rufus Keeler studied ceramic engineering at the University of Illinois, returning to California to work for Gladding McBean Tile Company in Lincoln. Here he worked as a ceramist developing clay bodies and glazes which would be compatible with the various clay bodies when fired. He soon became known as one of the best ceramic engineers in California. Keeler joined the California China Products Co. in National City, a suburb of San Diego, where he supervised the plant which produced tile for the 1915 Balboa Park Panama Exposition and the Santa Fe Train Depot in San Diego.

In 1916, Keeler moved his residence to Glendale, California and started his first ceramic facility, Southern California Clay Products Co., located at 2298 E. 52nd Street, Los Angeles. In 1923, Mr. Keeler reincorporated the business under the name of California Clay Products Co. (Calco), became the president and general manager, and built a new plant in South Gate, a few miles south of Los Angeles. Calco produced a full line of building and decorative tile products. Keeler built a beautiful home in South Gate utilizing extensive decorative ceramic tile in its

construction. He published an article featuring his South Gate home entitled, "The Use of Clay Products in the Modern Home," in the July 1925 *Bulletin of the American Ceramic Society.* In 1926, Keeler was commissioned by May K. Rindge to construct and operate the Malibu Potteries.

Some of the noteworthy projects Keeler supervised in the Los Angeles area prior to his career at Malibu Potteries included the Eastern Columbia Building at 9th and Broadway, the black and gold Richfield Building on Flower Street (replaced by the ARCO Towers), Exposition Park museums and the Uniroyal Building in the City of Commerce. While at Malibu, Keeler supervised the production of beautiful ceramic tile for the Los Angeles City Hall, Los Angeles Public Library, the Mayan Theater, the Rindge home in Malibu Canyon (now Serra Retreat), the Adamson home in Malibu Lagoon State Beach (now the Malibu Lagoon Museum), the Donald Douglas home in Santa Monica, and tile murals for Dana Junior High School in San Pedro. Malibu tile produced under his expertise and supervision can be found in many structures documented in photographs in this book.

The ceramic art of the Malibu Potteries resulted from the fortuitous combination of May Rindge's investment capital and commitment to excellence with dedicated employees functioning under the expert guidance of the gifted ceramist, Rufus B. Keeler. Keeler died on October 31, 1934 leaving a legacy of ceramic art to enhance the lives of future generations.

fig. 33

◄ fig. 32

fig. 34

fig. 35

fig. 32
1988 photo of tile floor entrance to Mayan Theater, Los Angeles showing durability. Detail of incised ornamentation still well defined after 60 years of heavy foot traffic. See figs. 33, 117.

fig. 33
1928 photo showing tile floor in entrance to Mayan Theater, Los Angeles. Note incised ornamentation (foreground). Vitrified brown clay body was used with various portions of the design being inlaid with different colored clays. See figs. 32, 117.

fig. 34
Maya fireplace inserts, 12" x 12," stock nos. B155 and B156 (p. 58 SPC). See fig. 35.

fig. 35
P. 58, Salesman's Pocket Catalogue, Maya inserts. See fig. 34.

19

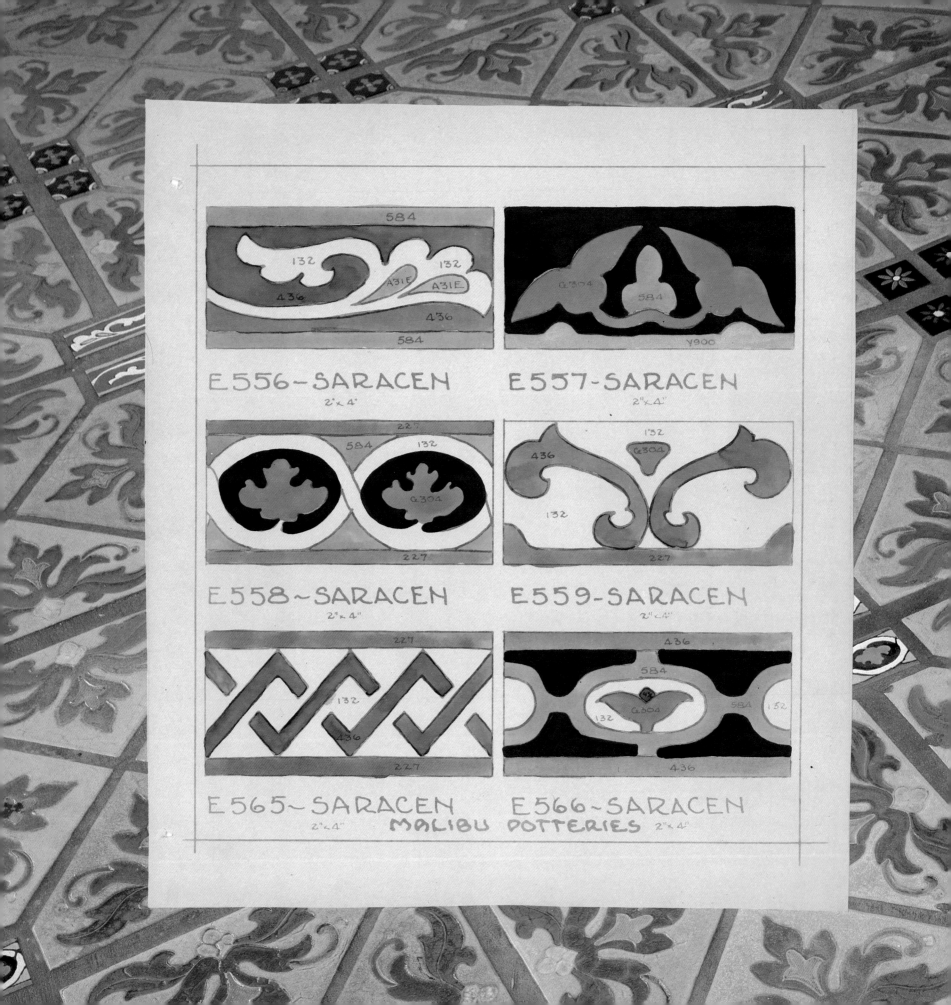

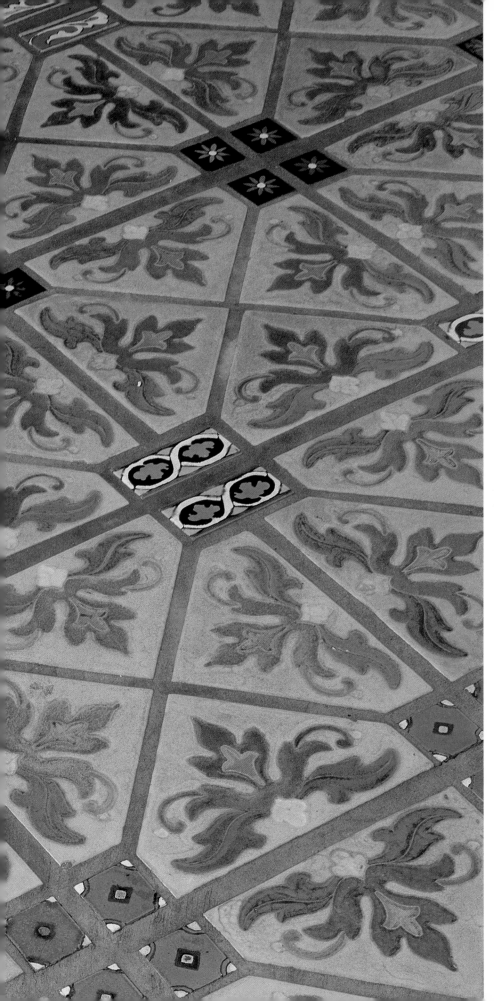

THE PLANT, DESIGN AND PRODUCTION

DESCRIPTION OF PLANT. The Malibu Potteries site was selected for its proximity to Santa Monica located not far from the east boundary of the Malibu Ranch. The Roosevelt Highway (now Pacific Coast Highway) had recently been completed from Santa Monica to Malibu. The highway made possible the employment of personnel living in the Santa Monica area and also facilitated the shipment of materials and products to and from the plant.

fig. 36
fig. 37

C H A P T E R   T H R E E

H igh-grade red and buff burning clays were abundant on the Malibu Ranch and were close to the site, much of it coming from Malibu Canyon. Water for domestic and manufacturing purposes was plentiful. The site was also located near Malibu Pier for possible shipping use.

Thus, in 1926, with an investment of approximately $250,000.00 the Marblehead Land Co., owned by May Rindge, constructed a plant to design and manufacture tile and other ceramic products. The plant was located on the beach about one-half mile east of Malibu Pier and occupied 44,000 square feet of floor space on a 1,500 foot strip of beach frontage. The buildings were constructed of brick made from local clays and roofed with corrugated steel with a saw-tooth profile which provided good lighting and ventilation for the employees. There was no telephone service and the nearest Post Office was in Santa Monica; for communications, a motorcycle messenger made daily trips to Santa Monica at noon. Gas and electricity were not available so a diesel generator was used to provide electrical power.

Fuel oil was brought in by truck and vaporized by air to fire three large updraft kilns which measured eighteen feet in diameter and had a total production capacity of 30,000 square feet of tile per month. One kiln was used for biscuit firing, one for glost (glaze) firing and the third was used for either—depending upon production needs. A smaller rectangular electric kiln was used for testing glazes and special projects.

THE DESIGN DEPARTMENT

The design department was located in a well-lighted room with large windows facing the ocean near the west end of the plant. Here drawings and sketches were prepared for the customer, who was often an architect or a builder. The location was inspiring to the designers who had a beautiful ocean view as they went about their work. Artists, trained in the technical branch of the business, designed tile products for the consumer. Many designs were taken from books and literature of decorative tile art. However, many magnificent patterns were original designs by the skilled artists at Malibu Potteries.

During the 1920's many California residences were constructed with exterior tile work, particularly around window and door openings. Other designs were needed for store and building fronts, including lobbies, domes, balconies, and courtyards which were often tiled.

Watercolor drawings of the stock tile were prepared in the design department for use by the salesman as catalogs for selling tile, as well as for use in production to illustrate the beautiful and intricate colors to be applied in glazing. Each glaze to be applied

22

overleaf
fig. 36
Watercolored page from Salesman's Scale Catalogue showing glaze color code numbers. See fig. 37.

fig. 37
Segment of entry floor to new dining hall at Serra Retreat, rebuilt after 1970 fire. Includes E96, E99, E556, E558. See fig. 36.

fig. 38

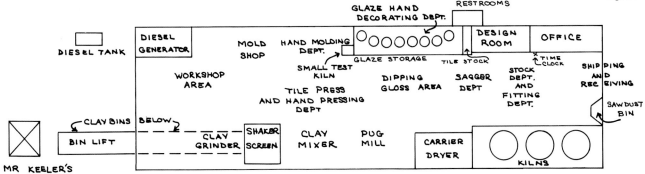

DIESEL TANK

DIESEL GENERATOR

MOLD SHOP

HAND MOLDING DEPT.

GLAZE HAND DECORATING DEPT.

RESTROOMS

DESIGN ROOM

OFFICE

SMALL TEST KILN

GLAZE STORAGE

TILE STOCK

TIME CLOCK

WORKSHOP AREA

DIPPING GLOSS AREA

SAGGER DEPT

STOCK DEPT. AND FITTING DEPT.

SHIPPING AND RECEIVING

TILE PRESS AND HAND PRESSING DEPT

MR KEELER'S TENT

CLAY BINS BELOW

BIN LIFT

CLAY GRINDER

SHAKER SCREEN

CLAY MIXER

PUG MILL

CARRIER DRYER

SAWDUST BIN

KILNS

fig. 39

fig. 38
View of Malibu Potteries on the beach between the Roosevelt Highway and the ocean, circa 1927. Note tent at left where manager R.B. Keeler lived during the week. The vents of the three large updraft kilns protrude from the roof at right of photo.

fig. 39
Map of factory layout, (not to scale). Derived from old photographs, descriptions by former employees, and the production process flow as interpreted by John. F. Rindge.

fig. 40
Photograph of the plant from the Coast State Highway (Roosevelt Highway), circa 1927.

23

fig. 40

fig. 41
Office and drafting personnel at work.

was indicated by a code number on the drawing which identified the glaze. Designs were traced from the drawings to the stencils which were prepared for applying the pattern on the surface of the tile. Stock designs were used in the preparation of a printed black and white catalog showing the complete line of tile patterns manufactured. See Chapter Five for sample catalog pages.

MANUFACTURING THE TILE

PROCESSING THE NEW CLAYS. Red and buff burning clays were hand dug and trucked from various sections of the Malibu Ranch to the pottery plant. Some Aberhill clays from Riverside County and English ball clays were purchased and used in the formulation of the clay bodies to give them plasticity and strength for pressing and handbuilding. The local clays

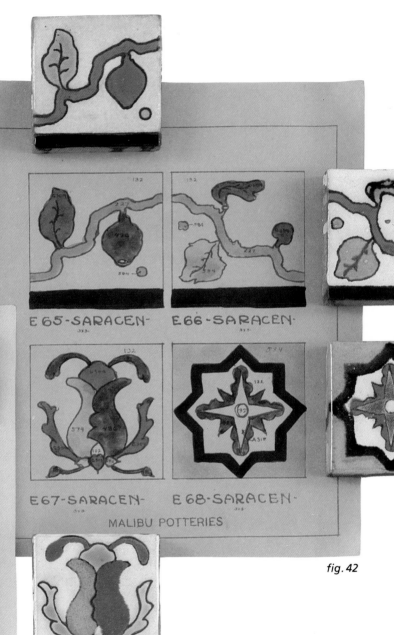

E 65 -SARACEN-

E 66 -SARACEN-

E 67 -SARACEN-

E 68 -SARACEN-

MALIBU POTTERIES

fig. 42

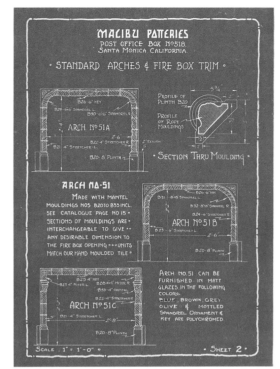

fig. 43

fig. 42
Watercolored pages from Salesman's Scale Catalogue showing glaze color code numbers with the corresponding Saracen production tile.

fig. 43
Blueprint, Standard Arches and Fire Box Trim, Sheet 2.

fig. 44
Indian head relief on plaque, 5" x 7½," made with clays of different hues. No glazes were used to achieve these colors.

were stored in bins and passed through a series of tests to determine tensile strength, color after burning, shrinkage, porosity, plasticity and hardness. A clay body formula was then followed for each separate clay batch used in the variety of tiles to be manufactured. Clay bodies were selected because of their burning color which ranged from buff to light brown to deep autumn reds and purple blacks. Each new batch was checked to insure quality control as the clay was processed.

The batches of clay were measured by dry weight and ground as fine as flour in a series of pulverizing machines; then the powdered clay was elevated in a four foot pan and dumped in a large bin where it was screened, removing any rocks, debris or larger

fig. 44

fig. 45
Auger machine for processing clay, similar to the type used at Malibu Potteries.

fig. 46
View of hand molding department.

fig. 47
View of kiln department showing the three large updraft kilns. Note sagger box held by worker in front of bricked door to kiln.

fig. 48
View of drying chamber where formed tile was dried prior to bisque (first) firing.

particles. The refined clay mix was placed in a disc type mixer and into a large auger machine where water was added to obtain the desired plasticity. The damp clay was placed in concrete storage bins where it remained for six weeks of aging. During this period the entire mass of clay became softened and uniform plasticity was attained. Just before the clay was taken to the pressers for forming into tile ware it was placed in a pug mill (an auger machine) to compact and work the clay and to remove any entrapped air.

FORMING THE TILE AND OTHER PRODUCTS. Many of the tiles produced were hand molded by placing the clay in plaster molds or hand shaping for special requirements. A spatula was often needed to assist in removing the tile from the plaster mold. Steel molds were used to form machine-made wall or floor tile. Two basic types of unfired tile were molded; one a flat smooth surfaced tile and the other a sculpted tile with a design impressed on the face of the tile. Large vases were formed by hand on the potter's wheel. Other products such as garden fountain bowls and chimney tops were pressed by hand into plaster molds. Special molds had to be made for custom orders. Fifty pieces of tile or terra cotta could be reproduced in one mold before the surface of the plaster became too pitted or worn for further use. Custom molds were made in as many as one hundred pieces to permit complex designs for architectural orders. These molds were retained for sixty days after the order was completed, and then destroyed.

DRYING THE WARE. It was necessary to remove the moisture from the ware after pressing, and great care was exercised to prevent the clay pieces from warping or cracking during the drying period. A large *Carrier* dryer was used to dry the tile in a separate room. This machine operated on a twelve to eighteen hour cycle: in the first stages of drying the humidity was maintained at a high level to allow pore spaces to open thereby permitting the moisture to evaporate in the latter stages of drying. During the drying stage the pieces would diminish in size due to loss of water; about half of the total contraction in size occurred. Special oil burning furnaces under thermostatic control were also used in the drying room. Each piece was laid separately on wooden pallets. These pallets remained under the piece from the time it was pressed until the time it was taken from the drying room, usually about 120 hours.

THE AMERICAN CLAY MACHINERY COMPANY

BUCYRUS   OHIO

American No. 329 Auger Machine

fig. 45

THE FIRST FIRING (THE BISCUIT OR BISQUE FIRE). The dry tiles were taken from the wood pallets and placed in saggers, made at the pottery, which measured 9½" wide, 14" long and 6¾" deep inside. (A sagger is an open box made from fireclay which has been previously fired). Harry Dellamore worked making saggers and recalls the process:

We spread the clay on a large, solid table. The table sides were one inch high, which was also the thickness of all sides of the saggers. We pounded the clay with an eight-inch wooden mallet until it was one inch thick. Marks on the side boards indicated where the sides of the sagger should be. The bottoms were made separately after the clay

fig. 48

fig. 46

27

had been pounded. The clay was then cut along the marks. We used a form to measure the inside of the sagger. We would roll the form on the table with one of the sides, join the two ends by working the clay with our fingers, then set the form on the bottom. Then we wet the sides where they join with the bottom and pressed the outside with our fingers. When the outside was finished, the form was taken out for working on the inside and the bottom. The sagger was put on a small pallet and set out for drying. After it had dried, it was fired and was ready to be loaded with a single layer of tile and sent to the kiln.[1]

fig. 47

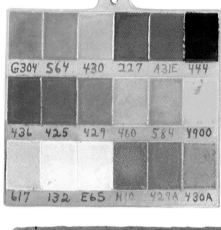

The loaded saggers weighed about sixty pounds and were set in stacks outside the kiln ready for placement in an empty kiln. Dellamore describes the loading procedure:

> There were three kilns. I helped load and unload them when extra help was needed. The saggers held newly-made tiles or bisc with a plain or color pattern. They arrived on the conveyor, and I would cover the top of the saggers with what we called "spaghetti" made from clay 1/2 inch thick. A small machine squeezed the clay out. Each sagger was covered so that when they were stacked one on top of the other, the spaghetti clay was pressed down and flattened to avoid leaks.[2]

E554 – SARACEN

fig. 51

The saggers were carefully stacked inside the kiln in concentric tiers about fourteen feet high, completely filling the interior of the kiln. The door opening of the kiln was bricked closed and sealed, and the fires lighted. The firing of bisque ware required ninety-six hours (4 days) and finished at a temperature of 2300° F. On the first day, the temperature was raised very gradually to allow the chemically combined moisture to escape from the tiles. At the end of

28

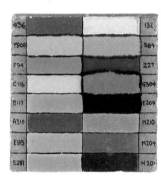

fig. 49

fig. 49
Production tile, E554.

fig. 50
Example of boards showing sample glaze colors from formulas developed by R. B. Keeler.

fig. 51
Watercolored page from Salesman's Scale Catalogue showing glaze color code numbers. See fig. 49.

fig. 50

the second day, the kiln began to redden as the temperature increased. During the third day the temperature increased even more rapidly. The interior chamber of the kiln could be viewed from various peep-holes. At the end of the fourth day, one could view the small pyrometric cones (1¾" high pyramids made of materials similar to a glaze, calculated to bend at a specific temperature), set in eight places throughout the kiln. When the cones had fused this indicated completion of the firing. Considerable training and experience were needed to fire the kiln, particularly in the latter stages. The kiln was allowed to cool for about two days and the bisque tile was then removed and placed in the biscuit stock department.

BISCUIT STOCK DEPARTMENT. Large quantities of stock-size tile were carefully laid out, sized and placed on the shelves in this department. Red burned tile and buff burned tile constituted the majority of the tile produced; some browns and dark colors were also produced and stocked in lesser quantities. Generally, bathroom tile used the buff bisque and decorative tile used the red bisque. Some of the bisque tile was ready for use as unglazed tile, but most of it was destined for glazing.

fig. 52

GLAZING

Glazes are similar to glass and are made from glass-forming materials, such as silica, alumina, soda, potash, zinc, lime, and lead with various mineral oxides added for coloring, such as iron (tan), copper (green), manganese (black), uranium (orange), nickel (brown), cobalt (blue), chromium (red), and antimony (yellow). These ingredients are mixed in a finely powdered form according to a pre-tested formula.

The glaze formulation was done only by Rufus Keeler who had spent years developing the glazes used. The glaze room was often referred to as "the holy of holies" because of the care taken to protect the formulation of the glazes and the written formulas as well. Potteries designer J. Donald Prouty talks about ceramics traditions regarding glaze formulation:

> In any ceramic plant, the raw materials used, the formula or recipe for the colors, the processing of them to the point where the glazes are a dry powder or an emulsion in water in crocks is a closely guarded secret, done behind locked doors. Traditionally, nothing is written down, but is passed orally from father to son. The area in the plant where glazes are formulated, from raw materials stored there, is strictly "off-limits" to all employees and visitors. Anyone trying to enter this area is dismissed and forever black-listed in the industry.[3]

The formulated glazes were stored as dry powder or as a water emulsion kept in covered crocks and identified by a code number. Constant diligence was required. If there was any uncertainty as to the contents of a glaze crock, it was dumped. Utensils were

fig. 52
Sagger box with tile after firing.

fig. 53

cleaned every time they were used. The formulated powdered glaze was mixed with water to the consistency of thick cream for application to the surface of the bisque tile. The glazes had to be the right thickness: if too thin, the color would be weak; if too thick, the colors would run together or overrun the tile. The creamy liquid glaze was applied to the face of the bisque tile by several methods: dipping, spraying or inlaying with fine tube syringes. The glaze was absorbed by the porous bisque as it was applied and soon dried on the surface of the tile, appearing as a thin layer of frosting on a cake. Donald Prouty noted the difficulties in distinguishing glazes by number only:

> None of them had the slightest resemblance to the final fired glaze, and all were so much alike that they could scarcely be distinguished one from another. For example: the rich deep black fired glaze was a delicate pale pink when applied to ornament a bisque.
>
> The artisans were practically working blind. Their only reference was the shop drawing with glaze numbers marked thereon which was before them.[4]

GLAZE APPLICATION METHODS. The most frequently used methods of glaze application were hand-dipping and inlaying with bulb-type syringes. Bisque tile glazed in a solid color was hand dipped by grasping the bottom edges and immersing the surface into the glaze to about half the thickness of the tile. If any glaze did run on the back of the tile it was scraped off before burning or ground

30

fig. 54

off after burning. The glazing of decorative tiles required that the design had to be first placed upon the bisque tile surface. When the design was a pictorial mural and all of the tiles were one of a kind, the outline drawing was prepared allowing spaces for the joints between the tiles. The outline drawing was traced on the bisque with carbon paper and a line of mixed manganese and oil was drawn with a small brush over the tracing on the surface of the tile. When the design was for tiles to be reproduced in large quantities, artisans in the factory would make a silk-screen stencil from the design department's line drawing. A heavy weight silk-thread mesh fabric was tightly stretched on a wood frame slightly larger than the tile.

The drawing was reproduced by filling the mesh of the screen with glue or shellac in all background areas, leaving the pores open only where there was a line on the drawing. The wood frame was hinged on a board with blocking to position the bisque tile directly under the design. Imprinting the design on the tile was done by forcing a paste-like manganese and oil mixture through the open pores in the mesh with a rubber squeegee. The stencil was then raised, the imprinted tile removed, and another blank bisque tile was inserted. An experienced operator could print a design every six seconds. Imprinted bisques were laid on a palette board and went directly to the glazing room.

fig. 53
View of hand decoration department, showing glazers using bulb syringes with tubes to inlay glazes onto the tile prior to the glost (second) firing. The windows at left look directly out on the Pacific ocean. The calendar on the far wall is dated October, 1926.

fig. 54
Enlargement of segment of photo in fig. 53 showing lady glazer using bulb syringe with tube to inlay glazes on the tile before her.

fig. 55

fig. 56

32

fig. 57

fig. 55
Cuerda seca method: dry black line separates glaze colors during firing. E17.

fig. 56
Cuenca method: impressed design in clay body of the tile forms ridges which separate glaze colors during firing. C39. See fig. 110.

fig. 57
Decorative bowl utilizing colors applied under a clear matt overglaze.

The manganese and oil mixture was a finely pulverized manganese oxide mixed with a medium viscosity mineral oil. The oil in the lines resisted the flow of the wet glaze placed in the spaces between the lines of the pattern in the design, leaving a dry line visible as the glazes dried on the surface of the tile. This process is known as the "cuerda seca" method meaning "dry cord" or "dry line", originally used by the Spanish and the Moors who used animal fats and grease instead of a mineral oil mixture. During the firing the oil burned off at a relatively low temperature; at a higher temperature, the manganese oxide fused and bubbled to form a charred dry line separating the glazes which were fired up to approximately 1900°F. When the tile was removed from the kiln the black line contrasted with the brilliant colors of the glazes complementing the over-all design. Another process of design called the "cuenca" (meaning "tub") method featured a design impressed into the surface of the wet clay tile with ridges serving as lines separating the glazes, thus forming tub-like areas where the glaze could be inlaid.

The glazes were put on the decorative tile by using a rubber bulb syringe with a glass or copper tube that had different size openings. A very fine-sized tube was used for small areas or details on the tile. The application of glazes in the designs outlined on the bisque formed by either the cuerda seca or cuenca process was entirely hand work, performed by artisans with steady hands and intense concentration. Some would complete only one tile at a time. Others were capable of glazing up to four or six adjoining tiles and completing all areas of one color before switching to another color until the

fig. 58

fig. 59

fig. 60

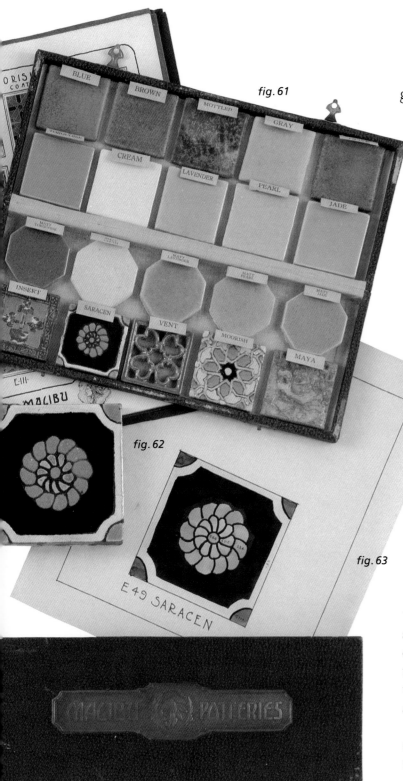

fig. 61

fig. 62

fig. 63

E 49 SARACEN

fig. 64

group of tiles was finished.

The glazers were seated on stools at a large "lazy susan" type wood-frame turntable measuring about 5 feet in diameter. The bisque tiles were placed on these turntables so that each artisan could easily rotate the table to the most convenient position for inlaying the glaze on the tile. The glaze decorating room was a large room with windows facing Malibu Beach and the Pacific Ocean. The artisans faced the ocean where they could enjoy the beautiful view. Plenty of natural light was provided from above through the row of windows in the upright section of the roof. In Chapter Four, Sarah Estrada Durant gives a detailed personal account of working in the glaze room.

Only when a large-quantity run was made of a stock pattern tile was any attempt made to assign a color to an artisan as her sole responsibility. Pallets containing six tiles were passed from one artisan to another until all areas were covered. There was no mechanical production line. The glaze inlayers were artists in their own right, assigned to the task at hand by a foreman according to their individual capabilities.

The rubber bulb syringe was filled with a glaze color mixture and used to flow glazes with a back and forth sweeping motion. Frequent agitation of the syringe was necessary to maintain an even flow. Tubes that clogged were freed with a thin wire probe and washed.

Brushes were sometimes used: small-size brushes were used to apply glazes from a pot or cup to

fig. 58
Standard Black and White Catalogue (9" x 11½") of 52 printed pages. See fig. 59.

fig. 59
Cover of Standard Catalogue, fig. 58.

fig. 60
Small (3¾" x 6¾") handpainted Salesman's Pocket Catalogue (SPC).

fig. 61
Salesman's Kit, 4½" x 11 ¼", with miniature tiles, one of which is E49. See fig. 62.

fig. 62
Production tile, E49. This is one of the 20 tiles in fig. 61. See fig. 61.

fig. 63
Watercolored page from Salesman's Scale Catalogue showing glaze color code numbers.

fig. 64
Cover of Salesman's Kit with miniature tiles. See fig. 61.

fig. 65
Original shipping crate with packing materials and tile.

33

fig. 65

tiny spots or areas of finely detailed designs; medium brushes were used for larger areas and big brushes (actually swabs) for solid color tiles and for finishing edges of tea tiles or border segments. Another method, underglazing, consisted of applying a pattern on the surface of the tile by stencil or brush, filling the areas with colored underglaze, and then applying a transparent overall glaze to the surface of the ware.

THE SECOND FIRING, THE GLAZE (OR GLOST) FIRE. After the tiles were glazed and dried, they were then placed in previously fired clay saggers. These were loaded into the kiln by hand and piled one on top of the other in concentric rings to a height of twelve feet. The glaze kiln capacity was about 5000 square feet of tile. Kiln loaders were constantly cautioned against using nails, washers, etc. in leveling the saggers placed in the kiln as the presence of iron in a kiln can spot an entire load of glazed products. Iron melts, vaporizes, and chemically reacts with the glazes if present during firing.

When the kiln was completely loaded with the saggers containing the tile, the kiln door was bricked and the fire was started. In fifteen hours the inside of the kiln began to redden, and in twenty-four hours the color was so bright that every detail within the kiln could be seen through the peep-holes. At the end of forty hours (at about 1900°F.) the pyrometric cones began to fuse and the fireman (kiln operator) reduced the fire to allow the heat to equalize throughout the mass of the load. The heat was held constant for about two hours and then shut off. The glaze fire required about forty-eight hours with an additional forty-eight hours required for cooling, a total cycle of four days.

An over-firing or under-firing, even if only in parts of the kiln, would alter the appearance of the glaze and make the ware worthless. For this reason, great care was taken to be sure that the temperatures were even throughout the load. Only an expert fireman was considered capable of handling the glaze firing of the kiln.

THE FINISHED PRODUCT

When the kiln was cool the brick door was taken down, and the saggers containing the tile were removed and unloaded. Great spectator interest was centered on the roller conveyors carrying the bright, beautiful tile. Each sagger brought forth a colorful surprise! Donald Prouty describes a lucky accident:

> The chemical reaction of glazes at the point of fusing sometimes produces interesting results. Part of a kiln load of high gloss glazed objects would be partly matte or with a crystalline pattern. I remember one instance where plain tiles intended to be a rich blue came out with crystals of bright orange scattered unevenly across the blue. It took nearly three months of experimentation to reproduce the effect on a controlled basis.[5]

The fired glazed tiles were then sorted into boxes near the kiln doors and taken to the stock department where certain tile products were laid out in panels or architectural forms and measured before being packed. Other tiles intended for bathrooms, mantels and bulkheads were carefully checked for color and size, then placed in stock for future shipments.

The finished product was carefully laid out in the Fitting Department and checked as to color, size and design. Defective or imperfect tiles were destroyed and new ones were made to take their place.

Fireplace mantels were crated together and each piece numbered according to the blueprint furnished with each order. Large doorways, pediments, and garden fountains were laid out for careful inspection prior to crating.

CRATING AND SHIPPING THE WARE. The last thing done was to check the ware as to quantity, color and size, and carefully pack the tile in sawdust in wood barrels or crates for shipment. A list of the contents was tacked on one side of the barrel or crate and each container was carefully labeled as to its destination. Shipments were made using the pottery's own trucks to the railroad depot at Santa Monica, where the tile was loaded onto rail cars for distant destination points.

SALES. A warehouse and sales display office was located in Los Angeles at 119 No. Larchmont Boulevard, just south of Beverly Boulevard. Tile was sold from this location to tile contractors and architects. Salesmen worked out of this office and called on their customers. In addition to selling the standard product line of tile, they coordinated custom orders with the plant in Malibu, working with the designers and artisans there. Salesmen were provided with a small fiber suitcase which would carry about 35 pounds of stock tile samples and a small kit of miniature tiles (See Kingsley Sopp's description in Chapter Four). Also, drawings of tile were painted with watercolors true to the glazes used, and these served as color portfolios in presentations to prospective customers.

PRODUCTS MANUFACTURED. A complete line of tile was manufactured for almost every architectural need. Among the products made were floor, wall, fireplace tile; tile for fountains, perforated ventilator tile, garden table-top tile, tile murals, stair treads and risers. In addition, other clay products were produced such as soapholders, towel hooks, chimney tops, large urns, railing balustrades, and specially designed ceramic pieces for architectural accents on buildings. On a very small scale the Potteries also produced ashtrays, bookends, small vases, decorative plates, cups, "tea tiles," smoking stands, and lamp bases.

However, most of the production of Malibu Potteries was devoted to tile. Two of the main product lines were the "Saracen" and "Moorish" designs. The "Saracen" line featured bright glossy glazes applied in the cuerda seca technique. The "Moorish" line featured both bright and matte glazed tile, the intricate patterns applied primarily with the cuenca method. Both of these lines of tile were multi-colored and predominantly geometric in abstract patterns, many featuring stylized flower, vine, and other plant motifs.

In addition to the highly decorative Saracen and Moorish lines, the Potteries also produced large quantities of floor, fireplace and mantel tile in a variety of patterns. Both glazed and unglazed red quarry and vitrified brown floor tiles were made using careful clay preparation methods combined with very high firing, making the tile non-slip and virtually indestructible. Hand-molded, Mayan-design fireplace and mantel inserts were produced in soft "Maya" shades of brown and green.

The tiles created by Malibu Potteries are among the most intricate, beautiful and well-executed tile ever made – a legacy of one of the most outstanding ceramic manufacturers in California history.

fig. 66
Advertisement in California Arts and Architecture.

fig. 67
Business card with Indian head logo.

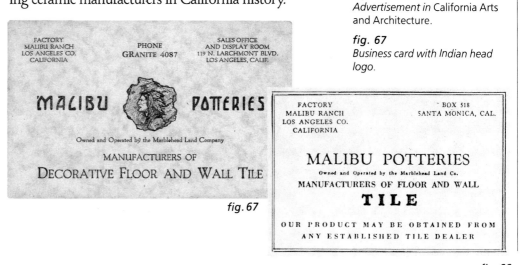

fig. 67

fig. 66

THE PEOPLE OF MALIBU POTTERIES

T HE CHARACTER AND AURA of any organization can be more fully appreciated by exploring the lives of the people who comprise that organization. Even though Malibu Potteries closed over 50 years ago, we are fortunate to have interviewed or corresponded with a number of former employees (or their relatives) who produced the ceramic art of Malibu Potteries in their idyllic factory by the sea.

fig. 68
fig. 69

CHAPTER FOUR

38

LILLIAN ABELL BALL
Glazer, Secretary, Bookkeeper

I was born in Buffalo, New York in 1903. My father worked for a lithographer who moved from Buffalo to Dunkirk, New York in 1909. I went to work for the lithographer where I met Donald Ball. After Don moved to Los Angeles in August, 1921, I followed in October and we were married.

In 1922, I went to work for California Clay Products Company (Calco) which was owned by Rufus B. Keeler. While at Calco I worked in the plant and also conducted tours for visitors.

I went to work at Malibu Potteries in 1926 when Mr. Keeler began hiring people to start the operation. At the time, I lived at 85th Place near Broadway. I commuted to Malibu with Pete Veltre, a presser at the plant, who picked me up at Manchester and Broadway. There was a gate and fence at Las Flores Canyon with guards there on horseback to let you through. The coast highway was often very bad to drive on at times due to the mud slides.

My first job at Malibu Potteries was working in the glaze room for Leo Hernandez. I then went to work in the office for Mr. Noonan, the bookkeeper for the plant, figuring the payroll and typing invoices. After a brief leave of absence in 1927, I resumed working at Malibu as Mr. Keeler's secretary. However, since Mrs. Rindge wanted someone who took shorthand, I returned to the glaze room working for Leo Hernandez. When the bookkeeper resigned to return to Cleveland, Mrs. Rindge asked that I return to the office to do the bookkeeping. With the help of Mr. Gowan, the bookkeeper for Marblehead Land Company, and several accounting courses, I was able to do the work.

During my time in the glaze room, I had charge of four girls who glazed the fancy tiles. I helped Leo mix glazes which had to be the right thickness; if too thin, you would not get the color you needed – if too thick, the colors would run into each other. The glazes were put on the decorative tile by using a rubber bulb and a glass tube that had different size openings. Leo would heat the glass tubing and pull it to make the kind of opening we needed for certain tiles. A very small opening in the glass tube was necessary for applying the glaze to the small places on the tile. The tubes would break and wear out so Leo was always making new ones for us. Solid color tiles were dipped in the color wanted.

I met Mrs. Rindge – everyone was afraid of her. I also met Mrs. Adamson (Rhoda Rindge Adamson). I was never in the Adamson home but did go up to Mrs. Rindge's home on the hill several times. I remember the Persian rug – it was just beautiful.

Some of us would go horseback riding about once a month after work. Mr. Keeler had a canoe and took two or three people out through the waves on calm days. Often on Sundays we would go to Malibu to go swimming and a number of us would swim over to the pier – it was such fun!

I worked at Malibu Potteries until the plant burned down on November 11, 1931. Don and I lived next door to Mrs. Keeler in South Gate until 1942 when Don passed away. I sold our home and returned to New York in 1947 where I worked in production control for Allegheny Ludlum Steel Co. in Dunkirk until I retired in 1963.

GLEN DAWSON
Plant Production

The late Glen Dawson worked at Malibu Potteries in 1931. The information which follows is based on a personal interview with Mr. Dawson by Ronald L. Rindge on May 21, 1984, and a personal letter to

Mr. Rindge from Mr. Dawson posted on June 19, 1984. Shortly after writing this letter, Mr. Dawson passed away. We are grateful to have direct information from this very knowledgable and delightful man. Born at the turn of the century, he was 84 years old at the time he was interviewed, but his mind remained sharp and expressive.

Glen Dawson worked primarily in preparing and handling the clay body as it went through the production process from raw materials to formed ware ready for the first or "bisque" firing.

Mr. Dawson recalled that the inside of molds were brushed with a green soap by the pressers to facilitate the removal of the formed tile ware from the molds. He recalled that the three large updraft kilns at Malibu Potteries were *never* left alone when in use. Experienced "burn" employees took turns watching the kilns at night, Saturdays, Sundays and holidays in addition to the normal work week. Mr. Dawson remembered several visits to Malibu Potteries by May K. Rindge whom he described as a tall and very dignified lady. He told of one instance when the department foreman told some of his employees to stay out of sight when Mrs. Rindge came to visit. Apparently, the foreman thought he had too many employees that day for the work going on in his department. Dawson spoke also of seeing Mrs. Rindge's yacht, *Malibu,* at anchor off Malibu Pier, and instances of wild packs of dogs chasing deer into the ocean.

After leaving Malibu Potteries, Glen Dawson worked for Fred and Florence Roberts in maintenance and as a refrigeration expert for the Roberts Markets and Liquor Stores. He also assisted the Roberts family in building the small dam in Solstice Canyon in Malibu to serve the water needs of the Roberts Ranch.

HARRY DELLAMORE
Plant Production

At 18 years of age, I quit school to work for a large plumbing supply company. Rufus Keeler lived close by and asked my Dad and I if we would like to come to the Malibu Potteries and install the finish plumbing in the building. We agreed.

We drove out as far as Las Flores Canyon where we were met by the Rindge property guards. The highway was still under construction, and we drove on the left near the ocean.

When we had completed the plumbing job, I asked Charles E. Mason, the Plant Superintendent, if I could stay and work in the Potteries. He gave me the O.K., and my first job was to stack the bags of casting cement and clay products that had arrived at the plant. Next, I was sent into a stationary boiler to clean the flues.

My main job was making saggers with W. W. Price (see Chapter Three for a description of this process). I had several other jobs at the Malibu Potteries. Each time a tank of oil arrived, it was dumped in a lower tank, and I pumped it to a higher tank to give more pressure to push the oil to the kilns. I would fire up the upright boiler, which was about 300 feet north of the plant and up on the side of a hill. I had to fire it with wood until I had the steam pressure up, then I could turn on the oil and fire with it.

I hauled tile up to the Rindge Mansion that was being built, and to Santa Monica. Twice, I drove a dump truck up north about ten miles for a special type of sand to be mixed with clay. For this I had help. I went on a delivery in an Adohr Dairy truck (Adohr Dairies was owned by Rhoda Rindge Adamson and her husband Merritt Adamson), carrying five tons of tile for a swimming pool at Monterey High School. I also blew the whistle to call people in from lunch, as

fig. 71
Harry Dellamore with wife, Gunda, enjoying Sunday at the beach, July 17, 1927.

many of them ate outside on nice days.

My last job at the Potteries was operating the grinding machine. I shoveled the clay into the grinder, which had two large solid wheels, six inches wide and about 30 inches high, that would rotate and crush the lumps of dry clay. The fine powder would fall through a grate, and scoops on a belt would carry the powder up to the shaker screen. Anything too large to go through the screen would drop down into the grinder again.

From the grinder, the clay was sent to the molding department, then on to the pressing department. The pressing was done with the hand, and excess clay was cut with a piano wire strung across a tight frame. The pressed tile was put on a tray that fit on a cart with wheels. In the pressing department was the machine that could make large tile and roofing tile by changing the die.

At very busy times, I helped out in the glaze room glazing tiles for the day. I also had charge of a crew that made roofing tiles for the Rindge home. As the tile came out of the roofing tile machine, one man would give it a little gray spray. Then we would shape and form the tiles a little with our fingers to make them look like hand-made tiles.

When I visited the Adamson House I remembered the days at Malibu Potteries. They were very happy times in my life. I had a car, wife, a good job and everything was great.

SARAH ESTRADA DURANT
Glazer

I was only fourteen years old when I started work at the Malibu Potteries. A truant officer from Santa Monica High School came to find out why I was not attending class and I told him I was working to support myself. He helped me obtain a work permit and put my age down as sixteen. I had lost my parents at a very early age, and lived with Mrs. Ignacia Ortega, whose brother-in-law, Jesus Mireles, did the transfer of patterns onto the tiles at the Malibu Potteries. Jesus brought me to work on special orders in the glazing department for a few months at a time in 1927, 1928 and 1929.

A special table was set up under the supervision of Leo Hernandez, the head of the Glazing Department. I punched a time clock at 7:00 a.m., put on my apron, and worked until noon. We would bring our lunch and sit outside to eat. In the afternoon, the women continued to work from 1:00 to 3:00 p.m. But the men worked until 4:00 p.m., so we would sit on the beach or walk while we waited for our carpool ride home.

Before the tiles came to the glazing department, the patterns were stenciled onto them. I used to watch Jesus Mireles create the stencils at his home. He would do many at one time, and was paid one dollar per stencil.

He would begin by tracing the patterns onto tracing paper. The tracing was then placed under silk organdy material which he had previously cut to fit a particular size frame. The pattern was traced once again onto the material. He then dipped this into a solution [usually glue or shellac] and waited for it to dry. When the material was dry, he would place it in the frame. With the tip of a knife, he then traced the outline on both sides of the silk material. The hardened solution came off easily, leaving only the design or pattern on the material.

Jesus Mireles transferred the stenciled patterns to the tile. He placed the tile in the center of the table with the stencil design on top. The frame fit into a special slot. He used a foot-controlled pedal to lift the frame up, leaving the stencil pattern on top of the tile. He would then brush a black ink-like solution on the

fig. 72
Sarah Estrada Durant at age 14, one of the youngest glazers.

silkscreen that became the stencil design on the tile. The stenciled tiles were placed in racks to dry. Each rack held ten to twelve tiles. When the tiles were dry, Jesus would move them from his left to his right side, so we would know they were ready for glazing.

I sat at the round glazing table with a pan of water on a chair at my side. Before glazing, the tile was dipped in water. The tiles dried almost immediately and were placed in double rows on the revolving table. With the pattern tile before me, I would arrange two rows of tile below it. I could look at the color numbers on the pattern and do two tiles in the same color quickly before turning the table. Each glazer would dip her bulb in the paint barrel, add a little water if necessary, and shake the bulb well. The bulbs were made of very soft rubber and were easy to use. Then, a yellow metal hook – made of brass, I believe – was inserted and the paint tested for consistency. With the bulb, hook and paint, we worked all the tiles in one color. To change colors, we washed out the bulb and hook and started the process over with new paint until the pattern was finished.

When all the tiles had been painted, they were placed on a pallet. Six or seven pallets would fit on a cart that was wheeled to the kilns. I estimate that I completed 150 to 200 tiles per day, depending on their size (3″ × 3″ or 4″ × 4″, and fewer if they were larger).

I remember working on a mural of Spanish dancers for Twentieth Century Fox Studios. These were full figures of a man and woman in color on a white background. I did very little painting with a brush, except for an occasional vase, ornamental dish, or a special cup. I have many fond memories of working at the Potteries and my friendships made there. Mr. Keeler, the Plant Manager, was very kind. One day he brought Mrs. Rindge to the glazing room and introduced me as "our Dolores Del Rio."

WILLIAM EDWARD HANDLEY
Draftsman, Artist, Designer

The following was written by William Edward Handley's son, James Allen Handley.

William Edward (Bill) Handley was the second of two sons born to upper middle-class parents in Halifax, Nova Scotia, on September 16, 1891. His father was a sea captain who ultimately went down with his ship in a North Atlantic storm. His mother was one of the Blackwell family, famous in the food industry as the producers of the well-known Cross-Blackwell jams and jellies.

The family moved to England where Bill and his brother completed their education. Bill received his degree in architectural design. At one time he also worked as an engraver.

After five years of service in the Canadian Army during the First World War, Bill returned to Canada where he married a Scottish woman who bore him two daughters and a son. When his youngest child was still a toddler, the family moved to the United States and settled in Santa Monica where they were close to his wife's family.

Being a small child at the time, I do not recall when my father started employment at Malibu Potteries, but he remained there in charge of designing until the pottery closed. He also worked for Taylor Tilery in Santa Monica. He stayed in the field of tile design until the start of the Second World War when he was hired at Northrop Aviation where he remained until after the war. He then entered the field of manufacturing tile and worked as plant manager

fig. 73

41

fig. 74

fig. 73
One of four jardinieres, Adamson House. 21″ bottom diameter, 14″ high, 29″ top diameter, cuerda seca technique. Designed by William E. Handley

fig. 74
Mural in butler's pantry, Adamson House. E630P. Designed by William E. Handley. Mural is bordered on left and right by tiles E704, E705.

for various tile manufacturing companies. Bill Handley died in his early seventies.

Margaret Curtis Smith, designer and illustrator, remembers her training under Bill Handley:

> Bill was English and had studied art in London. He told me the first rule of all professional potters is to pronounce "kiln" as "KILL."... I had never studied art, and Bill taught me how to fill space with graceful lines and beautiful colors. He taught me how to mix the paints so they matched the colors of the glazes. He even showed me how to sharpen a pencil properly.[1]

Margaret Smith also reported that it was Handley who designed the Dutch tile panels for the laundry of the Rindge mansion (still remaining at Serra Retreat), as well as jardinieres, the butlers pantry mural, and the Persian carpet for the Adamson house.

J. DONALD PROUTY
DOROTHY ALBRIGHT PROUTY
Designer and Secretary

The following information is based on correspondence between the late J. Donald Prouty and Ronald L. Rindge, supplemented by later correspondence with Mrs. Dorothy Prouty. Inez (Johnson) von Hake, a long-time friend of Don and Dorothy Prouty (all three worked for the Malibu Potteries), put Mr. Rindge in touch with Mr. Prouty. A number of letters were exchanged between them in February and March, 1981, concerning Prouty's experiences at Malibu Potteries and his major project—the designing of twenty-three large, decorative tile panels for the 1928 Los Angeles City Hall. Chapter VI relates Prouty's extensive work on the City Hall Project.

J. Donald Prouty was born in 1904 in Evanston, Illinois. His father was a Pullman conductor but Donald Prouty was able to study architec-

ture graduating Phi Beta Kappa from the University of Illinois in 1927. He married Dorothy Albright, a farmer's daughter born in 1906 in Rossville, Illinois.

Prouty tells how he first became aware of the Malibu Potteries while he was still a student:

> As a result of my thesis, "Color in Architecture", which won the Ricker Prize in Architectural History in 1925, I was employed as assistant to Rexford Newcomb, Professor of Architectural History. Under him I did illustrations for the magazine, "Western Architecture", of which he was the editor, and for the series of "Architectural Monographs on Tiles and Tile Work", which he was writing for the Associated Tile Manufacturers, Beaver Falls, Pennsylvania. This was a group of 13 eastern tile manufacturers...
>
> [The monographs] must have come to the attention of the Malibu Potteries management. Professor Newcomb received a letter in 1926 from R.B. Keeler and a box of assorted decorative tiles to show the work being done there. After an exchange of correspondence, Mr. Keeler offered Prof. Newcomb a position with Malibu Potteries. He declined the offer recommending me for the job.
>
> Mr. Keeler then wrote to me but his letter mentioned neither the scope of the work nor the salary. I wrote Mr. Keeler that I was interested, presented my credentials and asked what my responsibility and salary would be. This began a correspondence and series of events that could have been one of Robert Benchley's humorous articles. Mr. Keeler replied, naming a salary that was satisfactory, but instead of outlining my responsibility, he described the beautiful view of the surf and the foothills from the office windows. I accepted the salary offered and wrote him that I would appreciate the view, but surely the job was more demanding than looking out of the windows. Mr. Keeler's reply raised the salary offer by $25.00 per month, and instead of a job description, he wrote several pages of history of the Malibu Ranch, located north (west) of Santa Monica. I wrote again about my elusive duties and inquired into

fig. 75
Donald Prouty with his wife, Dorothy.

public transportation (to Malibu): was there a street car, bus line or railroad? Mr. Keeler's reply was that no transportation existed, and advised that I would need an automobile for which he raised the salary by another $25.00. I again thanked him and asked what my responsibilities would be and when they would start. Mr. Keeler's reply was terse and to the point: "Come at once."

I then wrote that I could not do so, because I still had eight months study to complete my degree, and I declined the job regretfully. Mr. Keeler then wrote that the job would be held open for me until mid-July of 1927. On June 1, 1927, I wrote him that graduation day had been set as June 15, that we had tickets and Pullman reservations made, and would arrive in Los Angeles at the Santa Fe Depot at 10:00 a.m., June 27, and asked that someone from Malibu meet us as this was our first visit to California.

While en route I sent a telegram from Denver on June 25 confirming our arrival on June 27 and again asked to be met in Los Angeles. You guessed it; there was no one to meet us, the phone company said there was no phone at Santa Monica or at the Potteries. Marblehead Land Co. admitted ownership of Malibu but merely referred me to a warehouse near Hollywood. The warehouse said they had no way to reach the Potteries but offered to take a message or me there the next day when a truck was scheduled to make a pick-up at Malibu.

We went to a hotel and the next morning I found my way via street cars to the warehouse, and rode on the truck to Malibu. Mr. Keeler said he had misplaced my letter, hadn't received the telegram, and was too busy to show me around Santa Monica or take me back to L.A. He handed me business cards of a realtor and used car dealer, and said: "Come back when you get settled." I returned via the truck and street cars and rejoined my wife at the hotel. The next morning, June 29, we rode on the Pacific

Electric line to Santa Monica, made arrangements to purchase an automobile, opened a bank account, and returned to the hotel on the P.E.R.R. The next morning we moved our bags and baggage by the Electric Line to our new home at 1425 1/2 Berkeley Street, Santa Monica, took possession of a 1924 Model T Ford roadster and spent the rest of June 30 learning to drive.

On the morning of July 1, 1927, I reported for duty at Malibu Potteries and was taken on a tour of the factory by Mr. Keeler and introduced to the two artists, Florence Hinchman and Inez Johnson, who later married a telephone company worker, Carl von Hake.

Thus began my two years association with Malibu. About three months later, Mr. Keeler asked me if my wife, Dorothy, did secretarial work. I assured him she was an experienced secretary and I would ask her if she would leave her present job to come to Malibu but her decision would depend on the salary. Mr. Keeler told me what the office job paid. When I informed Dorothy at home that evening—she immediately went to the phone, called the newspaper at Pacific Palisades and quit her job there. The next morning she packed one big lunch instead of two and rode with me to Malibu.[2]

Mr. Prouty confirms that Rufus Keeler stayed on the premises at night. He also relates an experience Keeler described and an incident he and Inez (Johnson) von Hake witnessed, both relevant to the contraband liquor activities in the late 1920's along the isolated Malibu coast:

There was a tent with a wood platform floor on the beach beyond the factory building and Mr. Keeler did stay on the premises Monday thru Friday, going home to South Gate on weekends during the two years we were at Malibu. It is entirely possible that he did so for the six years of the plant's existence. Mr. Keeler also had a "hidey hole" with a cot in it right up under the eaves above the stock bins and the shipping room (Jimmy Struck's department)—presumably used during bad weather.[3]

We heard of several incidents in the past and of one during our tenure at Malibu where liquor was landed in quantity through the surf at night during the dark of the moon, and carried to/or across the road into the hills. Mr. Keeler . . . said he observed an incident and hid until it was over because the participants were armed. Tracks across the sand—cut fences, etc. gave no clue to the disposition of the contraband. The Volstead Act, 18th Amendment, commonly called "Prohibition" was in effect at that time and illicit traffic was big business.[4]

fig. 76
7' x 13' tile mural at Dana High School, San Pedro, depicting Richard Henry Dana's ship, "The Pilgrim." Three hundred sixty-four 6" x 6" tile, cuerda seca technique. See J. Donald Prouty and Kingsley Sopp, Chapter Four. See fig. 78.

fig. 76

One morning Prouty and Inez von Hake found the body of a murdered man uncovered by the tide. In a brief newspaper account:

It was mentioned that this was another of the killings attributed to the bootlegging gangs. In his book, Mr.

Frederick H. Rindge mentions smugglers landing at Malibu from sailing ships offshore during the early days. It was still occurring in the 1920's![5]

Asked to describe his work as a top designer, including any research required and how he generally spent his working days, Mr. Prouty provided the following comments:

My approach to designing tiles for a specific use was to:

1. Determine the architectural style and period of the building in order that the ornamentation be compatible.

2. Determine the distance from which the tiles would be seen in order to set the "scale." (Example: a design small in scale and highly colored would be charming in a small room. The same design outside the building where it would be viewed from a distance of 20 feet or more would be seen as a general tone and gray color—entirely unsuitable.)

3. Then by reference to architectural design sources proceed to detail the tiles and determine the colors of glazes to be used.

I had done intensive research on tile with Prof. Newcomb as previously mentioned. We had at the University of Illinois in Urbana and in museums and architectural libraries in Chicago access to the finest books on design and tile work. These were not available in Los Angeles and my contemporaries in the architectural offices there had only limited books usually not available when needed. To bring the design resources at Malibu up to the highly respected position it was gaining in the faience tile industry, I suggested that consideration be given to starting a reference library here. I furnished Mr. Keeler with a list of books known to me. Mr. Keeler took this to Marblehead Land Co. and much to his surprise, and mine, Mrs. Rindge approved the idea. It took nearly three months for dealers and agents to track down copies of these works before almost all books requested were received. They were so valuable, money wise, that a safe to hold them was also purchased. Malibu then had a very definitive reference library. Mrs. Rindge's largesse in this instance was a marked contrast to her handling of the weekly requisition for supplies for the office and studio and stamps for mailing. These were blue pencilled drastically by Mrs. Rindge or someone at Marblehead Land Co. We seldom received more than half of what was needed.

Let me describe a typical day for me at Malibu. When I was in the office I usually started the day by reviewing with the artists the work they were doing in making water color renderings for approval of clients of proposed use of our stock tiles on specific projects. Then I would check and assemble such finished renderings with sample stock tiles, bill of material, etc. for use of either our salesmen or the dealers. New requests for such presentation drawings were organized by me. If stock tiles could be used I would select appropriate tiles and make a free hand layout for guidance of the artists. If the project required special designs, I would proceed to make a 3/4" to 1'0" scale rendering in color for client's approval. When it was approved and Malibu had the order, I would full size the drawings for the individual tiles for the use of the factory—an outline only if the design for use in transferring it to the bisque and a color drawing bearing our glaze numbers for the use of the glazers. Each individual design was assigned a number, and a 3/4" scale blueprint of the entire project would be prepared to show the location of each tile in the project. This "setting diagram" was used to check the finished tiles before shipping, and by the tile setters who would install them.

One of the first custom design projects I did for Malibu Potteries was the mural of a sailing ship and the companion map of the California coast which were installed in the Dana High School (San Pedro, CA). I did the small scale presentation drawings and setting diagrams, and the full size line and color drawings from which these

panels were made by the factory. When the project originated, the old map submitted by the high school was suitable for reproduction in tile, but their print of the ship left much to be desired. From my personal copy of Two Years Before the Mast, illustrated by Howard Pyle, I developed a view of Dana's ship that was authentic historically and better adapted to the mural.[6]

In answer to a question about a "brick factory" on the north side of the highway between the factory and Malibu pier, Mr. Prouty responded:

The abandoned brick yard north of the pottery on the land side of the highway right-of-way was not in operation during my two year tenure at Malibu. It was located at the local clay deposits and undoubtedly was the source of the red common brick used in building the three large original kilns in the plant. The yellow clay saggers and setting slabs probably were also made there and possibly the original fire clay or vitreous liners of the kilns as well. I don't believe any of the bricks were sold elsewhere, and, once the new kilns were built in the potteries, all needed items could be produced there.[7]

Mr. Prouty describes the circumstances of his leaving Malibu Potteries, his subsequent career in the Southern California tile industry, and later, as an architect in Chicago:

Dorothy and I left Malibu Potteries together in July or August, 1929, when the first shutdown was termed a "temporary layoff"...[8]

[We] found other work within a few days to tide us over the layoff, and did not return to Malibu when it eventually re-opened a few months later that year. By that time, we had found other (full-time) employment.[9]

Dorothy became secretary to the Gilfillan Bros. Radio Corp. of Los Angeles. I first went to work for Gladding McBean, under Jesse E. Stanton, A.I.A., where I was *designer for the tile work for the Alexander & Baldwin (sugar brokers) office building in Honolulu. Then in March of 1930, I became designer and Architectural Liaison for Claycraft Potteries. I stayed there until the plant closed in March of 1932 as did other ceramic tile plants including Malibu. In the spring of 1933 I came to the realization that the tile industry was indeed dead, and moved to Chicago. I found a temporary job as Architect in the corporate headquarters of Montgomery Ward & Co. That temporary job lasted 36 years![10]*

Mr. Prouty continued to paint in Illinois: historic places, log cabins, pioneer farmsteads, landscapes and ghost towns he and Dorothy visited in the Southwest in the 1920's and 1930's. He won many art awards. In 1975, Don and Dorothy moved from Chicago to Bellefontaine, Ohio. In 1979, for the fourth consecutive year, Mr. Prouty's art was selected as one of the 10 "Best of Show" awards in the Governor's Art Show in Columbus, Ohio.

J. Donald Prouty died in the fall of 1982, leaving his ceramic art and award-winning paintings as testimony of a full, creative life that will enrich the lives of all those who view his work in generations to come.

ELEANOR PARKER RORICK
Glazer, Watercolorist

As a first-year student at Santa Monica High School, I spent the summer break in 1928 working at the Malibu Potteries. Although the stock market crash was yet to come, we were already in the clutches of the Great Depression. I had to work.

Rufus Keeler, a friend of friends, found a spot for me in the glaze room, where I learned to inlay glaze. I lived with my family in Santa Monica, and because there was no transportation along the coastal road in those days, I rode to Malibu in a car pool. The drive to the Potteries took about half an hour.

At 7:00 a.m., a whistle was blown to signal the beginning of our work day. I entered the plant at the east end. The glaze room was large with a number of round tables. The tiles, with designs already outlined, were laid out on the periphery of the tables which could revolve as the glazer laid on one color at a time. Leo Hernandez, the glaze man and foreman, would supply us with the proper colors for each part of the design. All the raw glazes were a whitish color, indistinguishable one from another. We were very careful not to use the wrong colors. Only after firing did the true colors show.

Although I liked the work, it was sedentary and tedious. On occasion I would doze off, and when word got to Mr. Keeler, he arranged for me to go swimming during the lunch hour. This refreshed me for the rest of the day's work. Once while swimming at Crystal Beach (Venice-Santa Monica area), I saw a young man holding someone in the water. I had just completed a lifesaving class at the Edgewater Beach Club, so I swam the man in to the beach with an overarm carry. I later learned that he was taking part in a fraternity outing and received thanks from all the fraternity brothers.

Mr. Keeler encouraged me in my work and suggested excellent books for me to read. He also arranged for me to learn how to do the watercolor illustrations that were used in the catalogues the salesmen carried. I think it was William Handley who instructed me. It was exacting work, but while working, one could look out upon the ocean.

Mr. Keeler mixed the glazes, and Leo Hernandez was the head of the glazing department. Remembrance of those times past is kept alive for me by the tile work in the Adamson house, some of which is my own glaze work, including the series of ships on the ceramic walls of the son's bathroom upstairs. The more elaborate work, such as the Persian rug in the loggia, was not done by the production crew, but by the more experienced craftsmen. There was always excitement in the air when these special projects were under way, especially when we were allowed to visit the Adamson residence to see installations in progress.

MARGARET CURTIS SMITH
Designer and Illustrator

One of my assignments as a senior at Huntington Park High School in 1929 was a 3,000-word term paper on an industry of my choice. My next door neighbor, IB Young, was employed at Malibu Potteries, and I asked him if he could arrange for me to tour the plant. IB spoke to Rufus B. Keeler, manager of the Potteries, who very kindly took me through the plant and explained the workings in great detail. Mr. Keeler also lent me some of his valuable books on the history and manufacture of tile and some portfolios of beautiful reproductions of Persian tile panels.

I hand-lettered all 3,000 words of the paper and drew tile patterns down the sides of the pages and on the cover. Not only did I get an A+ from my teacher, but Mr. Keeler, upon seeing my work, offered me a job at the Malibu Potteries for a year between high school and college. Although I was untrained in design, I had drawn and painted school projects, so I learned easily with the support and encouragement of Mr. Keeler and William E. Handley (Bill), the head draftsman and designer.

I started work on Saturday, June 15, 1929 – the day after I graduated from high school. I was 17 years old, and my salary was $20.00 for a forty-four hour week. The women worked from 7 a.m. to 3 p.m., and the men from 7 a.m. to 4 p.m. We also worked four hours on Saturday. Since I lived two hours from Malibu with my widowed mother, Mr.

Keeler made arrangements for us to rent a charming room close by in the home of Bill Handley's sister-in-law.

My first project was a large plate, about 18 inches in diameter, that Bill Handley had sketched on tracing paper. The design of flowers and leaves was very loose, and Bill told me to "finish" it. He explained that the stems had to be at least ¼ inch wide, as the glaze syringe could not flow the glaze into a narrower space. With Bill's suggestions, I made the color designs.

I painted renderings of floors, wainscots, panels, all for the approval of clients. I also drew "stock tile" designs for the catalogue books used by the salesmen. The catalogue pages were reproduced in a "brown line presentation" by a blue print company. I cut the pages, rounded the corners, punched the loose-leaf holes for the books, and numbered the pages. The colors in the catalogue had to match the tiles exactly, so the customer could make the proper selection. When the illustrations had all been painted, they were shellacked for protection and to give them the appearance of real tile. It took a week to prepare and paint the basic 36-page catalogue, to which we would add more pages of new designs. Often when I was working on a catalogue, Bill would bring me a tile and say, "Put the book away and paint a wainscot using this tile."

As I remember, the catalogue pages were 8″ × 10″ and beige in color, which enhanced the finished painting. The rendering would be about 4½″ high and 5″ or 6″ wide, the scale being ½ inch to a foot. The squares representing the tiles were penciled in lightly, using T-square and angle. Then the design was painted free-hand. We used opaque Catalina Colors to simulate tile. Sometimes we used Winsor & Newton water colors.

Oftentimes, I referred to Speltz' *Styles of Orna-*

ment or the *Handbook of Ornament* by F.S. Meyer when asked to make a design in a certain style. When we had a number of new designs and color schemes to be added to the catalogue, I drew them in reduced size using India ink onto the blue gel material used to make the brown line prints. Mr. Keeler or Bill Handley selected these designs.

I also created new color schemes for old tile to bring them up to date by using new glazes developed by the chemist. The chemist worked in a rectangular area, about 20′ × 10′, completely enclosed, top and sides, with heavy wire. There was a lock on the door. Glaze formulas were very secret and belonged to the person who created them.

I created and drew the designs on six jars for the Roman bath for one of Mrs. Rindge's sons. One jar had clusters of poinsettias with green leaves on a white background. Another had a cluster of chrysanthemums and was white with grey shading on a light blue background. There were small white Chinese clouds scattered around. Two more had Saracen designs on an ochre background. I believe there were birds and fish on the others.

I painted many renderings of floors, some using glazed inserts and tile risers, wainscots, soda fountain counters, fountains, wall panels, and bathroom trim.

Lillian Ball, the bookkeeper, Inez von Hake, an artist, and I swam almost every day of the year—hot or cold, rain or shine. When the surf was rough, Mr. Keeler acted as our life guard. I will always remember my year at the Malibu Potteries. I left in the middle of August, 1930 to attend college in Ohio. When I returned, I worked in two other potteries, as the Malibu Potteries was closed. I am most grateful to my two friends and mentors, Rufus B. Keeler and William E. Handley, for inspiring the artist in me and for their support and kindness.

fig. 77
Kingsley Sopp, salesman. Photo taken at Adamson House, March 26, 1977.

KINGSLEY SOPP
Salesman

The late Kingsley Sopp was employed by Malibu Potteries in February 1927 as a salesman. Driving his 1925 Chevrolet roadster, he worked out of the company's Los Angeles display room on Larchmont Boulevard, calling on architects. He worked only three months at Malibu Potteries, but describes his sales duties in a very interesting letter to John F. Rindge dated September 3, 1973:

> During the time I worked for Malibu, I called on almost every listed architect in Los Angeles, Pasadena, Beverly Hills, Long Beach and Santa Ana. I had a small fiber suitcase that I could pack about 35 pounds of samples into and a briefcase in which I carried four hand-painted catalogues. They were done in water colors and were very true to color.
>
> It was fun calling on the architects. Most had a day or half-day they would receive material salesmen. Many times they would tell me they would give me 10 minutes. After I opened my sample case and catalogues, it was a different story. They would begin to call their draftsmen out and then show me projects they had on the boards ranging from schools to commercial buildings and residences. It usually took from an hour to 1½ hours, and often I was given a print and asked to have our art department submit a design for portions of the building, ranging from arches, stair-risers, fountains and benches. Everything was Spanish architecture in those days.
>
> On large jobs, I would obtain a set of plans and drive to the plant to discuss them with Mr. Keeler. He was a master of design and would outline the tile for their artist to use in his drawing. During my time there, we supplied the tile for the Donald Douglas home. Also, I was called to the Santa Monica Tile Contractors Showroom to assist Gloria Swanson select the tile for her home.

In a letter to John Rindge dated March 22, 1974, Mr. Sopp describes his involvement in the creation of two colorful tile murals for the Dana Junior High School in San Pedro:

One of the most important jobs using Malibu tile I worked on was the Richard Henry Dana Junior High School in San Pedro. I was the leg man between the art department at Malibu and Mr. Nibecker, the chief architect for the Los Angeles School Board. His specification called for two scenic panels of tile, one on each side of the entrance: one depicting a nautical map of San Pedro at the time Dana visited, and another the sailing ship he came in (the Pilgrim).

I made several trips to the Los Angeles Library to their old map section and found one of San Pedro at that time (1834). There was no harbor as such then. Ships anchored outside in deep water and their freight was loaded into small boats and rowed into port. I traced the map along with all the flying dolphins and characters those early maps were decorated with and took it to our art department—also a picture of his four masted schooner.

Our art department made a sketch of each about 18″ × 20″ and I took them to architect Nibecker. He was delighted with them and approved them at once. In fact, he called all of his draftsmen in to see them. I believe the panels were 6 ft. by 8 ft. From these sketches full sized production drawings were made so the design could be transferred to the bisque.

I saw the job about 8 years ago (1966) and it was beautiful. I was proud and thankful for the small part I had in it.

Mr. Sopp writes of his abrupt departure from Malibu Potteries in his letter dated September 3, 1973:

Then one Monday morning I walked into my desk and an envelope lay there from the Marblehead Land Co and it contained a check for two weeks pay in advance and a note stating that my services would no longer be required. Our sales manager insisted I go with him down to see Mr. Keeler for an explanation. He was as surprised as we were but said one did not question motives—that during the three years he had been there she had fired 11 ranch foremen and they got no explanation either.

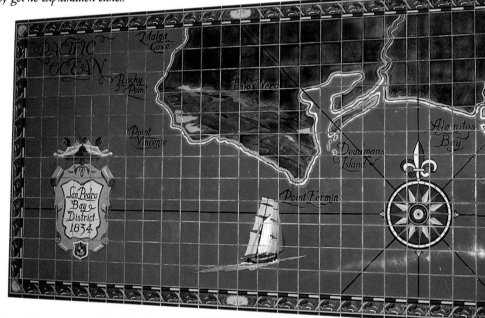

fig. 78

After leaving Malibu Potteries in 1927, Mr. Sopp went on to other companies in the ceramic industry, eventually retiring as Vice President and General Manager of Pomona Tile Company. At the invitation of the Malibu Historical Society, Mr. Sopp and his wife, Bess, toured the Adamson house and grounds at Malibu Lagoon State Beach on March 26, 1977. In a letter dated April 3, 1977 to Ron Rindge, Mr. Sopp commented about this visit:

Bess and I had a most enjoyable day and were privileged to visit the Adamson home. I had not seen many installations of the tile, and certainly none so elaborate and complete as that was.

Mr. Sopp passed away on September 23, 1984.

fig. 78
7′ x 13′ tile mural at Dana High School, San Pedro, depicting San Pedro Bay in 1834. Three hundred sixty-four 6″ x 6″ tile, cuerda seca technique. See J. Donald Prouty and Kingsley Sopp, Chapter Four. See fig. 76.

fig. 80 ▶

fig. 79
Inez Johnson von Hake, designer and illustrator, employed at Malibu Potteries from 1927 to 1932.

fig. 80
The 13' x 59' Persian carpet made of tile laid out on the floor of Malibu Potteries before installation in Mrs. Rindge's mansion. A simulated braided silk fringe in tile (F1, fig. 113) was added to the ends of this carpet when it was actually installed at Serra Retreat. The first impression is that of a priceless oriental rug. See figs. 195, 203, 206.

INEZ (JOHNSON) VON HAKE
Designer, Illustrator

My memories of the Malibu Potteries date back to 1927. I was living with my parents in Ocean Park, now a part of Santa Monica. The Potteries advertised for a sculptor. Douglas Burden, a talented sculptress, was interested but she did not feel like going so far alone and asked me to go with her.

The plant was built on the beach, a short distance east of the Malibu Pier—a most beautiful and unusual location for any kind of industry. At that time, the low speed limit along the two-lane coastal road made the trip seem much longer than it is today. I went with my friend, and that was my introduction to the Malibu Potteries.

Rufus Keeler, manager of the plant, hired Douglas Burden, only to have her leave after a few days. Douglas told me later that the noisy surroundings of the clay pressing and other plant activities disturbed her. That same day, Mr. Keeler offered me work in the glaze room. I had no idea what that would involve, but after he took us to the glaze room, I declined his offer. I could not see myself sitting all day, squeezing liquid glaze colors from a syringe onto tiles. He then asked if I would be interested in working in the drafting room, in case of an opening there. I told him that I would be interested, if I could qualify.

Sometime later, Mr. Keeler asked me to make drawings from some rough sketches for 8" × 8" tiles. I made the designs at home, and when he saw them, he offered me a job in the design department. That was the beginning of my five years at the Malibu Potteries—1927 to 1932.

J. Donald Prouty from Illinois was the outstanding artist at Malibu Potteries. The Potteries furnished a good deal of tile for the new Los Angeles City Hall in 1928 and Don designed some exceptional panels and lunettes. He also made small scale drawings of all tiles in stock. These included colorful designs of Saracen, Moroccan and Espanol tiles, and Mayan inserts, in bold relief, which were glazed with matt neutral brown and olive green. Other illustrations were made of stock accessories, moldings, lunch counters, and special-order swimming pool tiles.

Brown line prints were made from Don's drawings, and I water-colored all the decorative designs except for the Mayan inserts. For preservation, I varnished each design which added a realistic appearance. The finished product went into small catalogues which were used by salesmen and architects. The 3¾" × 6¾" pages were placed in a loose-leaf binder. Four pages with rounded corners were printed on a sheet with six circles for punching printed on each page. I used a paper cutter to separate the pages, but had to hand cut the curved edges. I punched the holes and assembled the pages in the binders. Terms and conditions of sale, net prices, etc., were placed in the back of the book.

I made water-color sketches for special orders. These were suggested designs for storefront bulkheads and wainscots, showing the use of all decorative or plain tile, with decorative stock tile. I also made original Persian-style designs. Among these were a large plate, a curved console table top, and a 2 × 4 foot table top, made especially for the Adamson Beach House. This was set in the ornate wrought-iron table located in the entry hall.

My last and most challenging assignment was to design the Persian rug, 13 × 59 feet, for the loggia of the Rindge Mansion, which later became Serra Retreat. Because of the awkward dimensions, Mr. Keeler suggested a large rug with smaller ones at each end. However, Stiles Clements, the architect from Morgan, Walls, and Clements, preferred one rug. A special huge drawing board was set up at one end of the drafting room. I stood on a long bench in order to

reach the upper section of the board, which was higher than my 5'1" height.

I selected patterns and motifs and began by sketching the pattern on tracing paper at the scale of ¾ inch to one foot. I used very wide drawing paper on a big roll. I chose my own color scheme and painted half the design in Winsor & Newton watercolors from England. When I had completed the design, José and Jesus Mireles transferred the pattern from my drawing to the bisque tile. I then numbered the design colors on my drawing which went to the glaze room. Leo Hernandez and Mr. Keeler worked together on the glazing. Mr. Keeler chose a matte glaze finish for the tiles. The 879 tiles were 12" × 12" with 6" × 12" borders, and 6" × 6" at the corners. Each tile was an inch thick.

Frequently during the noon hours, we would go swimming. The men worked nine hours a day, with a half hour for lunch. Women were not allowed to work over eight hours in one day, so we had a longer time for swimming or just relaxation. I have many happy memories of those days and the times we spent together.

The Great Depression caused the Malibu Potteries to shut down in 1932. Only a few employees remained to complete unfilled orders. I had not completed the full-size drawing of the rug and told Mr. Keeler that I would like to finish it at home on my own time. Mr. Keeler permitted me to take my small-scale color rendering and other materials to finish the full-size drawing.

A few days later, Mr. Keeler called me. He had told Mrs. Rindge what I was doing and, to my surprise, she asked me to return to work. She said, "Anyone that interested in her work should be kept on the payroll." I was delighted because I felt certain *then* that Mrs. Rindge intended to have the rug produced. One

day when I was alone working on the rug, she came into the drafting room. She was very friendly. I shall never forget that brief visit with her.

I was very excited when Mr. Keeler invited me to see the completed rug. My father, mother, mother-in-law, and a friend went with me. Mr. Keeler had the tiles taken straight from the kiln and laid out in a section of the plant that had been cleared and cleaned after the 1931 fire had swept through the building and burned the roof down. He placed a ladder at the center of the rug to enable us to get, as Mr. Keeler said, "a bird's-eye view."

On August 1, 1962, the Franciscan Order held an open house at Serra Retreat for a benefit project. I went with Florence La Gatta (wife of artist John La Gatta), my daughter, Margaret, and my sister, Ruth Yaphe. The Franciscan Brothers were the tour guides.

Before entering the loggia, our guide said, "Now, ladies and gentlemen, you are about to see the outstanding feature of Serra Retreat – a Persian design tile rug, designed by an artist who was brought in from India." My sister quickly said, " Would you like to meet the designer?" With a most astonished look, the guide answered, "Indeed I would." She then introduced me, and he said, "We were told that a man came from India to design the rug." A lady turned to me and said, "This is my second tour, and that's what they are telling everyone." She asked for my autograph – a new experience for me.

We entered the loggia. The rug in that gorgeous setting was much more spectacular than when I had first seen it at the fire-damaged Malibu Potteries. It was magnificent! I realized more than ever before the truth of the saying, "A task accomplished and happiness are inseparable." Designing that rug was the biggest task I had ever undertaken. I had worked 60 days on it, and I enjoyed every minute of it.

fig. 81

53

fig. 81
*A beach day at Malibu Potteries,
circa 1928.*

fig. 82
*Saracen panel, E22-P. 1' x 1'6".
See fig. 139*

fig. 83
*Saracen panel, E23-P. 1' x 1'6".
See fig. 139.*

fig. 84
Saracen panel, E62-P. 6" x 1'.

fig. 82   *fig. 83*

fig. 84

The following names are those of persons known to have worked at Malibu Potteries sometime during the period 1926-1932. Most of the names are from a roster of employees dated January 1927.

W.M. **Acton**, bisc stock
Elmer **Afner**, kiln setter
Howard **Afner**, kiln setter
Enrique **Aguilar**, kiln setter
Henry **Aguilar**, dipper
E.A. **Alexander**, order clerk
Bruce **Anderson**, kiln foreman
John **Aracia**, mold maker
Katherine **Ashmead**, draftsman
Merrill W. **Baird**, draftsman
Robt. G. **Baldwin**, tracer
Lillian Abell **Ball**, invoice clerk
Earl **Ballinger**, dipper
Thos. E. **Bangs**, box maker
Henry **Beetlestone**, bisc stock
Mrs. Pearl **Bones**, glaze inlayer
G.W. **Borland**, glost stock
Roy **Brooks**, glaze stock foreman
Doug. (Ms) **Burden**, sculptor
P. **Burgess**, glaze stock
Minnie M. **Butler**, glaze inlayer
W. S. **Butler**, clean-up man
M.E. **Clark**, glaze inlayer
Ed **Connolly**, truck driver
Thos. H. **Conroy**, salesman
Margaret **Curtis (Smith)**, designer
Geo. D. **Custer**, inventory clerk
Ed. H. **Dahlgren**, packer
C.E. **Daniels**, engineer
Harry **Davis**, glaze stockman
Ray **Davis**, placer
Glen **Dawson**, clay man, presser
John **Davenport**, salesman
Joe S. **Deamer**, packer

Mrs. J. S. **Deamer**, glaze inlayer
Harry **Dellamore**, saggers
B. **Demovich**, presser
Darrell **Dryden**, kiln setter
P. **Dryden**, kiln setter
Mr. **Edwards**, Adamson house tile foreman
Sarah **Estrada (Durant)**, glaze inlayer
Clyde **Faust**, packing
Jennie **Fielder**, glaze inlayer
Forest **Fielder**, glazer
Wm. J. **Fisler**, bisc stock
Dean G. **Foster**, presser
R. L. **Gaxiola**, kiln setter
Elsie **Gill**, glaze inlayer
Clayton **Godlove**, presser
Mary **Godlove**, glaze inlayer
Ignacio **Gonzales**, presser
Lula **Gregg**, glaze inlayer
W.E. (Bill) **Handley**, designer
W.A. **Hanna**, glost stock
(Leo) **Hernandez**, glaze man
Carl **Heynen**, presser
Florence **Hinchman**, designer
John **Hopping**, placer
E. **James**, sagger repair
John **Jewell**, glaze stock
W. **Jewell**, glost stock
Inez **Johnson (von Hake)**, designer
Roy C. **Jones**, salesman
Atanas **Katchamakoff**, modeler
R.B. **Keeler**, manager
John **Kokal**, plaster man
Jas. **LaChimia**, glaze stock
Ralph **Leon**, glaze helper
E. **Lopez**, kiln setter
Frank **Lopez**, kiln setter
Ruperto **Lopez**, kiln setter
Emil **Lundstrom**, carpenter
Harry **Lundstrom**, shipping department

Katherin **Lurton,** glaze inlayer
Wm. **MacDonald,** night watchman
J.F. **MacDonald,** oiler
G.W. **MacKinnon,** salesman
John **MacPherson,** glost stock
Duane **Mapes,** finish stock
E.W. **Martin,** warehouseman
C.E. **Mason,** superintendent
Ernest **Mathewson,** presser
V.O. **McDaniel,** presser
Nellie **McDaniel,** glaze inlayer
T.L. **McGriff,** operator
Merrill **McIntire,** presser
Mr. **Meyers,** craftsman
A. **Micklosy,** welder
Frank J. **Miller,** presser
Tony **Milloglav,** presser
C. **Ming,** dry pan
Jesus **Mireles,** dipper
Jose **Mireles,** dipper
C.L. **Mix,** tile machine
Gertrude **Moore,** artist
Lily **Moothart,** glaze inlayer
Vonda **Moothart,** glaze inlayer
C.R. **Morgan,** truck driver
Carrie **Neff,** glaze inlayer
John **Nickerson,** modeler
D.L. **Noonan,** bookkeeper
Adeline **Nunez,** glaze inlayer
Amado **Nunez,** kiln setter
Ben **Nunez,** kiln setter
L.C. **O'Brien,** presser
Mrs. Minnie **O'Brien,** glaze inlayer
Mrs. C. (Elizabeth) **O'Handley,** placer
Mrs. Mary **Palmer,** glaze inlayer
Eleanor **Parker (Rorick),** glaze inlayer
H. **Peckham,** pressing foreman
Mr. **Pemberton** (father), draftsman
Wilmer **Pemberton** (son), draftsman
William T. **Poates,** presser
Jesus **Portillo,** clay dept.

W.W. **Price,** saggers
J. Donald **Prouty,** artist,designer
Dorothy **Prouty,** secretary
Wm. **Provost,** dipper
Henry **Ramerez,** clay man
George **Reynolds,** bisc stock
Kenneth **Richards,** kiln setter
Jesus **Rodriquez,** kiln setter
Manuel **Rueda,** dipper
B. **Sabine,** bisc stock
George **Seperica,** kiln setter
J.J. **Sheridan,** dipper
Edgar **Short,** presser
Tony **Smith,** glaze stock
Kingsley **Sopp,** salesman
Margaret **Stewart,** asst. tracer
J.N. **Struck,** bisc stock foreman
Chas. **Sweeton,** presser
Gertrude **Tasker,** glaze inlayer
Grover **Tasker,** presser
Carl **Thornton,** presser
Pat **Torao,** presser
Porifiro **Torres,** kiln setter
John **Tudor,** kiln setter
George **Ulyatt,** bisc stock
Mary L. **Ulyatt,** glaze inlayer
Pete **Veltre,** presser
Connie **West,** glaze inlayer
Walter A. **West,** packer
Paul **Williams,** kiln setter
IB **Young,** kiln burner
Robert **Young,** production
Mrs. Verna **Young,** glaze inlayer
Grace **Yordy,** glaze inlayer
L.A. **Yordy,** bisc stock

fig. 85

PRODUCTS OF MALIBU POTTERIES

MALIBU POTTERIES MANUFAC-TURED a complete line of tile for almost every architectural need. The following photographs illustrate the wide range of those products, including the large-volume Saracen and Moorish tile lines and some small-volume decorative ceramic items.

Most of the tile products were listed in two catalogues used by Malibu Potteries. The *Standard Catalogue,* was fifty-two pages. The small *Salesman's Pocket Catalogue* was a loose-leaf binder which contained many watercolored tile designs, some from the *Standard Catalogue* and some which were not.

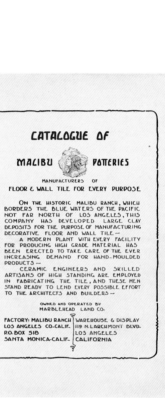

CHAPTER FIVE

CATALOGUE OF

MALIBU POTTERIES

MANUFACTURERS OF
FLOOR & WALL TILE FOR EVERY PURPOSE

ON THE HISTORIC MALIBU RANCH, WHICH BORDERS THE BLUE WATERS OF THE PACIFIC NOT FAR NORTH OF LOS ANGELES, THIS COMPANY HAS DEVELOPED LARGE CLAY DEPOSITS FOR THE PURPOSE OF MANUFACTURING DECORATIVE FLOOR AND WALL TILE.—
A MODERN PLANT WITH EVERY FACILITY FOR PRODUCING HIGH GRADE MATERIAL HAS BEEN ERECTED TO TAKE CARE OF THE EVER INCREASING DEMAND FOR HAND-MOULDED PRODUCTS.—
CERAMIC ENGINEERS AND SKILLED ARTISANS OF HIGH STANDING ARE EMPLOYED IN FABRICATING THE TILE, AND THESE MEN STAND READY TO LEND EVERY POSSIBLE EFFORT TO THE ARCHITECTS AND BUILDERS.—

OWNED AND OPERATED BY
MARBLEHEAD LAND CO.

FACTORY: MALIBU RANCH | WAREHOUSE & DISPLAY
LOS ANGELES CO.-CALIF. | 119 N. LARCHMONT BLVD.
P.O. BOX 518 | LOS ANGELES
SANTA MONICA-CALIF. | CALIFORNIA

fig. 86

fig. 87

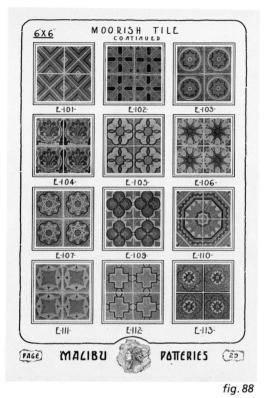

fig. 88

overleaf
fig. 85
A collage of tile produced by Malibu Potteries.

fig. 86
Title page and 3 Index pages, Standard Catalogue.

fig. 87
Stair-risers to south patio, Serra Retreat. In ascending order: E101, E104, E114, E18 E102, E106, E705, E111, E5.

fig. 88
Page 29, Standard Catalogue, Moorish tile. See fig. 87.

INDEX

BATHROOM FLOOR TILE (MATT GLAZED)
THE NEUTRAL COLORS OF THESE TILE BLEND WITH OUR BATHROOM WALL TILE.— VARIOUS SQUARE AND RECTANGULAR TILE AS WELL AS 4" OCTAGON AND HEXAGON TILE ARE CARRIED IN STOCK.— PAGE 10

BATHROOM WALL TILE (BRIGHT & MATT GLAZED)
THESE TILE POSSESS THE SUBTLE CHARM AND FINER QUALITIES WHICH CHARACTERIZE HAND-MOLDED PRODUCTS.— THE SURFACE IS SOFT AND UNDULATING, THE COLOR SHADED BY THE NATURAL FIRING, AND IN ALL RESEMBLING CLOSELY THE WORKMANSHIP OF EARLY PERIOD CRAFTSMEN.—
HARMONIOUS DESIGNS ARE SECURED BY THE USE OF TRIM, LINERS AND PANELS.—
BATHROOM ACCESSORIES IN ALL THE STANDARD SHAPES AND COLORS, INCLUDING DECORATIVE MALIBU DESIGNS, ARE CARRIED IN STOCK.— PAGES 4-9 11-13

FLOOR TILE (RED QUARRY UNGLAZED)
A FULL LINE OF RED QUARRY FLOOR TILE IS CARRIED ON HAND.— THE SIZES VARY FROM 2½" TO 12"x12" INCLUDING HEXAGONS AND OCTAGONS.—
THE RICH CHERRY RED COLOR OF THESE TILE IS ATTAINED THROUGH THE CAREFUL PREPARATION AND USE OF MALIBU CLAYS.— THE BURNING OF THE TILE RENDERS THEM NON-SLIP AND VERY HARD.— PRODUCING AN ATTRACTIVE COMBINATION OF SOFT SHADES.— PAGES 40-43

FLOOR TILE (VITRIFIED BROWN-GLAZED & UNGLAZED)
AUTUMN SHADES OF EXTREME SOFTNESS ARE PRODUCED DURING THE BURNING OF MALIBU CLAYS AND THE HARDNESS AND INDESTRUCTIBILITY OF THESE TILE IS WELL KNOWN.— THEIR USES VARY ACCORDING TO THE EFFECT DESIRED.— SIZES FROM 2" SQUARE AND UPWARD ARE STOCKED.— PAGES 44-46

FLOOR TILE INSERTS (DEPRESSIONS GLAZED)
RED QUARRIES WITH SARACEN AND MOORISH DESIGNS INCISED AND INLAID WITH COLORED GLAZE FORM A PORTION OF OUR FLOOR TILE STOCK.—
THESE INSERTS ARE USED WITH THE VITRIFIED BROWN AS WELL AS THE RED QUARRY FLOORS.— PAGE 45

FOUNTAIN TILE (BRIGHT & MATT GLAZED)
GLISTENING, BRILLIANT, COLORFUL MOORISH AND SARACEN TILE ASSEMBLED IN PATTERNS OF EXQUISITE BEAUTY AND EMBELLISHED WITH SPOUTING DOLPHINS, FROGS AND GROTESQUE HEADS ARE STOCKED PARTICULARLY FOR GARDEN OR PATIO DECORATION.— PAGES 50-51

INDEX
CONTINUED

LUNCH COUNTER TILE
COMBINATIONS OF VARIOUS SIZES AND COLORS ARE USED IN THE TREATMENT OF COUNTER FRONTS.—
WE CARRY VITRIFIED FOOT RESTS IN RED-BROWN COLOR FOR COUNTER WORK.— ALSO BRACKETS, DECORATIVE INSERTS, RAIL TRIM, ETC., GLAZED IN COLORS TO MATCH OUR STANDARD TILE.—
COUNTER FRONTS MAY BE MADE OF OUR MATT GLAZED MANTEL TILE, AND RICH, COLORFUL FRONTS ARE OBTAINED THRU THE USE OF OUR SARACEN OR MOORISH TILE.— PAGES 52-55

MANTEL TILE (MATT GLAZED)
THE TILE ARE RUSTIC IN APPEARANCE WITH ROUNDED CORNERS AND IRREGULAR SURFACES.—
THE RICHNESS OF COLOR TONE AND THE SUBDUED EFFECTS PRODUCED MAKE THE TILE VERY EFFECTIVE FOR INTERIOR TREATMENT.—
A LARGE ASSORTMENT OF INSERTS, BRACKETS, MOLDINGS, SHELVES, HOODS, HEARTH RISERS, ETC., ARE STOCKED TO MATCH.— PAGES 14-25

MAYA TILE (BRIGHT & MATT GLAZED)
REPLICAS OF THE ORIGINAL STONE CARVINGS OF PRIMATIVE AMERICAN PEOPLE ARE MADE, IN RUSTIC, ROCK FACED BLOCKS AND USED IN THE DECORATION OF MANTELS, WAINSCOTS, BUILDING FRONTS, FLOORS, ETC.—
MANTELS AND INSERTS OF THIS TYPE ARE CARRIED IN STOCK.— PAGES 57-58

MOORISH TILE (BRIGHT & MATT GLAZED)
HISPANO-MORESQUE DESIGNS INLAID OVER INTRICATE PATTERNS MOULDED IN CLAY FORM INTERESTING REPLICAS OF THE EARLY SPANISH DECORATOR.— A WIDE VARIETY OF DESIGNS IS ON HAND FOR IMMEDIATE SHIPMENT.— PAGES 29,32, 37-38

PERFORATED VENTILATORS (BRIGHT & MATT GLAZED)
VENTS ARE STOCKED IN VARIOUS SIZES AND COLORS.—
THE DESIGNS ARE DECORATIVE AND MAY BE APPLIED TO GRILLES, HEAT REGISTERS, VENTS, GARDEN WALLS, GATES, ETC.— PAGE 56

SARACEN TILE (INLAID ENAMELS)
THE ARCHITECTURE OF SOUTHERN EUROPE HAS BEEN DECIDEDLY INFLUENCED BY THE CERAMIC ART OF THE SARACENS.— FAITHFUL REPRODUCTIONS OF THEIR WORK ENABLE US TO CARRY OUT DESIGNS OF VARIED CHARACTER, INCLUDING GARDEN SEATS, TABLE TOPS, FOUNTAINS, PANELS, BORDER AND TRIM.—
WE STOCK SIZES FROM 2" SQUARE TO 6" SQUARE.— PAGES 26-28, 30-34, 35-39, 37-39, 56,61

INDEX
CONTINUED

STEP TREADS & RISERS (MATT OR UNGLAZED)
VITRIFIED BROWN BURNING CLAYS ARE MOLDED INTO VARIOUS TREADS AND RISERS, STAIR PLATFORMS OR TO FIT IRREGULAR AREAS.— THE LATTER ARE MADE TO ORDER ONLY.— THE EFFECTS PRODUCED ARE IN HARMONY WITH OUR VITRIFIED BROWN OR RED QUARRY FLOOR TILE.— PAGE 47

STORE FRONT TILE
MODERN ARCHITECTURAL DEVELOPMENT HAS MADE POSSIBLE THE USE OF COLORFUL AND DECORATIVE TILE STORE FRONTS.— BY THE SKILLFUL USE OF OUR VARI-COLORED UNITS IT IS POSSIBLE TO PRODUCE EFFECTS NEVER BEFORE ATTAINED IN THIS TYPE OF DECORATION.—
MINIATURE TERRA COTTA BLOCKS ARE ALSO MADE FOR USE IN CONNECTION WITH THESE TILE FRONTS.— PAGES 59-60

SPECIAL SHAPES (MISCELLANEOUS)
INNUMERABLE SHAPES FOR SWIMMING POOLS, GARDEN FURNITURE, TABLE TOPS, HAND RAILINGS, ARCHITECTURAL MOLDINGS, RELIEFS, PANELS, ETC., ARE EITHER STOCKED OR MADE TO ORDER.— PAGES 62-67

MALIBU PRODUCTS

WE ARE ENTERING AN ERA OF COLOR IN ARCHITECTURE WHICH REQUIRES CAREFUL STUDY OF EACH NEW PROBLEM AT HAND AND MAKES POSSIBLE COMPLETE INDIVIDUALITY AND REFINED DISTINCTION IN EVERY HOME.—
OUR PRODUCTS COMPRISE A WIDE VARIETY OF SHAPES, COLORS AND SIZES, BOTH GLAZED AND UNGLAZED, INLAID OR EMBOSSED; AND IN MATT OR SEMI-MATT FINISH.— WHICH IN ALL PRESENT UNLIMITED POSSIBILITIES TO THE DECORATOR.— DELICATE TINTS AND RICH WARM TONES CAN BE COMBINED TO EFFECT A CHARMING AND HARMONIOUS WHOLE.—
ONLY THE MOST CAREFULLY PREPARED CLAYS ARE USED IN OUR MANUFACTURING PROCESS, AND THE BURNING OF THE WARES IS CARRIED TO EXTREMELY HIGH TEMPERATURES TO INSURE PERMANENT AND INDESTRUCTIBLE TILE WHICH WILL FOREVER RETAIN THEIR ORIGINAL FRESHNESS AND LUSTROUS FINISH.—

E127

E134

E121

E164

E163

E166

E128

E123

E108

E101

E169

E146

E120

E115

E167

E167

E155

E144

E157

E145

E159

E154

E156

E150

E161

fig. 89

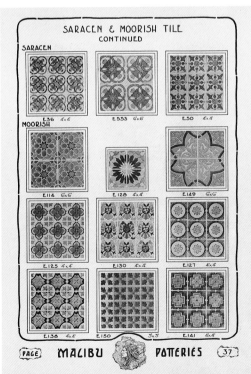

fig. 89
Assorted, identified Moorish tile.

fig. 90
Page 37, Standard Catalogue, Saracen and Moorish tile.

fig. 90

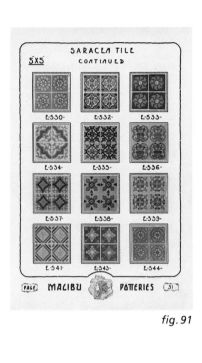

fig. 91

fig. 91
Page 31, Standard Catalogue,
Saracen tile.

fig. 92
Assorted, identified Saracen
tile.

fig. 93
Assorted, identified Saracen
tile.

fig. 94
Entry portal, chauffeur's room
and garage, off service
corridor, Adamson House. Includes E536, E528, E537, E527,
E612, E532, E530, E525.

fig. 95
Page 7, Salesman's Pocket
Catalogue.

fig. 92

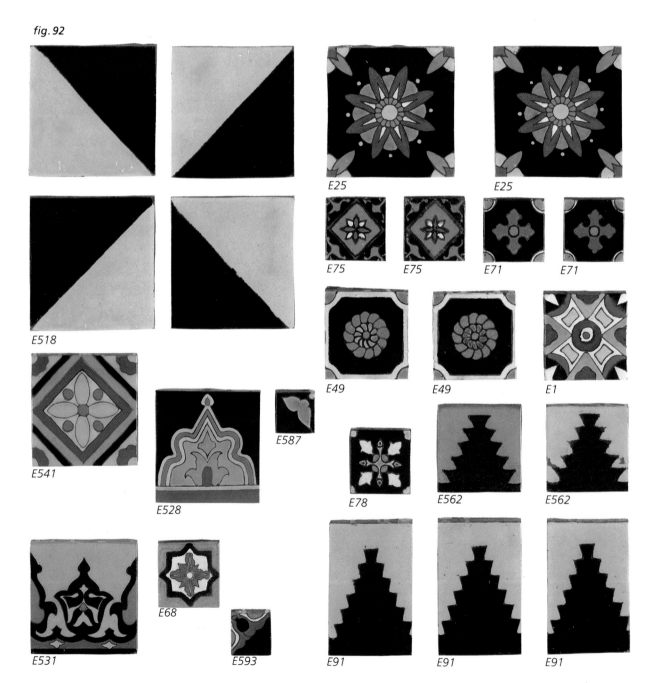

fig. 93

E584

E65

E66

E50

E50

fig. 94

E35

E53

E596

E41

E582,
miter

E551

E526

E34

E737A

E69

E539

E536

E534

E537

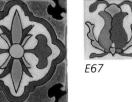

E532

E67

E529

E542

fig. 95

SARACEN TILE
5"x 5"

E 612   E 613

E 536   E 537

E 539   E 543

MALIBU POTTERIES

fig. 97

fig. 96

fig. 96
Bathroom, service corridor,
Adamson House.
Includes E70, E17, E43.

fig. 97
Nurse's bathroom, 2nd floor,
Adamson House. Includes E8,
E16, E68, E27.

fig. 98

E554

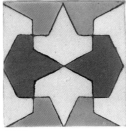

E589

fig. 100

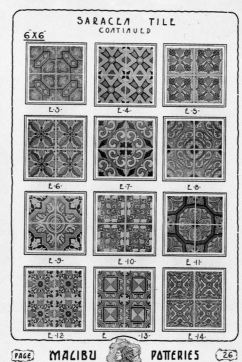

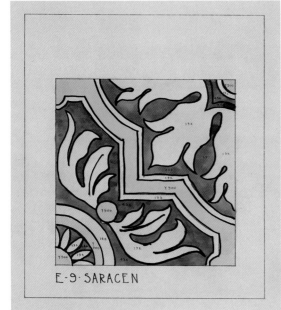

E-9·SARACEN

fig. 99

E19

E16

E9

E17

fig. 98
Assorted, identified Saracen tile.

fig. 99
Watercolored page from Salesman's Scale Catalogue showing glaze color code numbers. See figs. 98, 100.

fig. 100
P.26, Standard Catalogue, Saracen tile.

fig. 101
Tile bench, Adamson House, 2nd floor observation deck facing east. Includes E12, E16.

63

fig. 101

SARACEN TILE
2"x2" CONT.

E515 E587 E592 E593

3"x3"

E65 E66 E67

E68 E69 E70

E71 E72 E75

E76 E78 E79

MALIBU POTTERIES

fig. 102

fig. 103

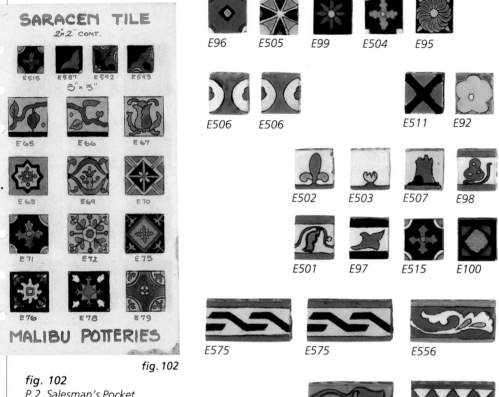

E96 E505 E99 E504 E95

E506 E506 E511 E92

E502 E503 E507 E98

E501 E97 E515 E100

E575 E575 E556

E576 E565

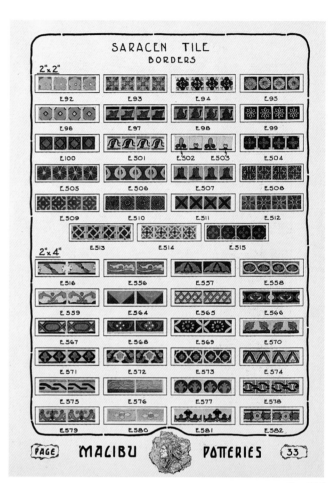

SARACEN TILE
BORDERS

2"x2"

E92 E93 E94 E95

E96 E97 E98 E99

E100 E501 E502 E503 E504

E505 E506 E507 E508

E509 E510 E511 E512

E513 E514 E515

2"x4"

E516 E556 E557 E558

E559 E564 E565 E566

E567 E568 E569 E570

E571 E572 E573 E574

E575 E576 E577 E578

E579 E580 E581 E582

PAGE **MALIBU POTTERIES** **33**

fig. 104

fig. 102
P.2, Salesman's Pocket
Catalogue, Saracen tile.

fig. 103
Assorted, identified Saracen
tile.

fig. 104
P.33, Standard Catalogue,
Saracen tile borders.

E567 E558 E568 E578 E559 E582

E564 E557 E570 E566 E579 E580

fig. 105

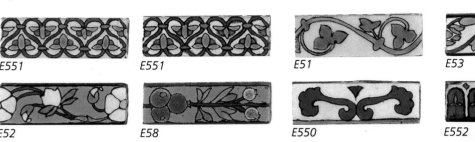

E551   E551   E51   E53

E52   E58   E550   E552

E546   E46

E549   E549

E28   E28

E560   E561

E65   E66   E522   E521

E41   E77   E67

fig. 106

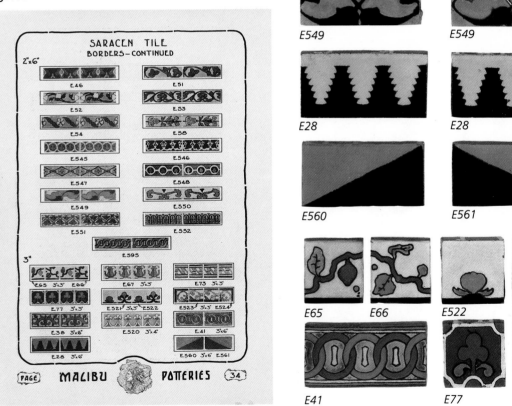

SARACEN TILE
BORDERS—CONTINUED

2"x6"

E46
E52
E54
E545
E547
E549
E551

E51
E53
E58
E546
E548
E550
E552

E595

3"

E65 3½×3 E66   E67 3½×3   E73 3½×3

E77 3½×3   E521 3½×3 E522   E523 3½×3 E524

E38 3½×6"   E520 3½×4"   E41 3½×6"

E28 3½×6"   E560 3½×6" E561

PAGE MALIBU POTTERIES 34

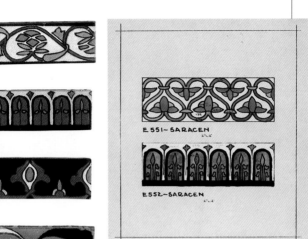

E551~SARACEN

E552~SARACEN

fig. 107

fig. 105
Assorted identified Saracen tile.

fig. 106
P.34, Standard Catalogue,
Saracen tile borders.

fig. 107
Watercolored page, Salesman's
Scale Catalogue, showing glaze
color code numbers. Stock
numbers E551, E552 are
in figs. 105 and 106.

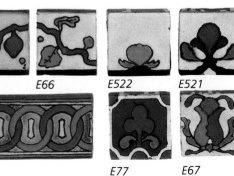

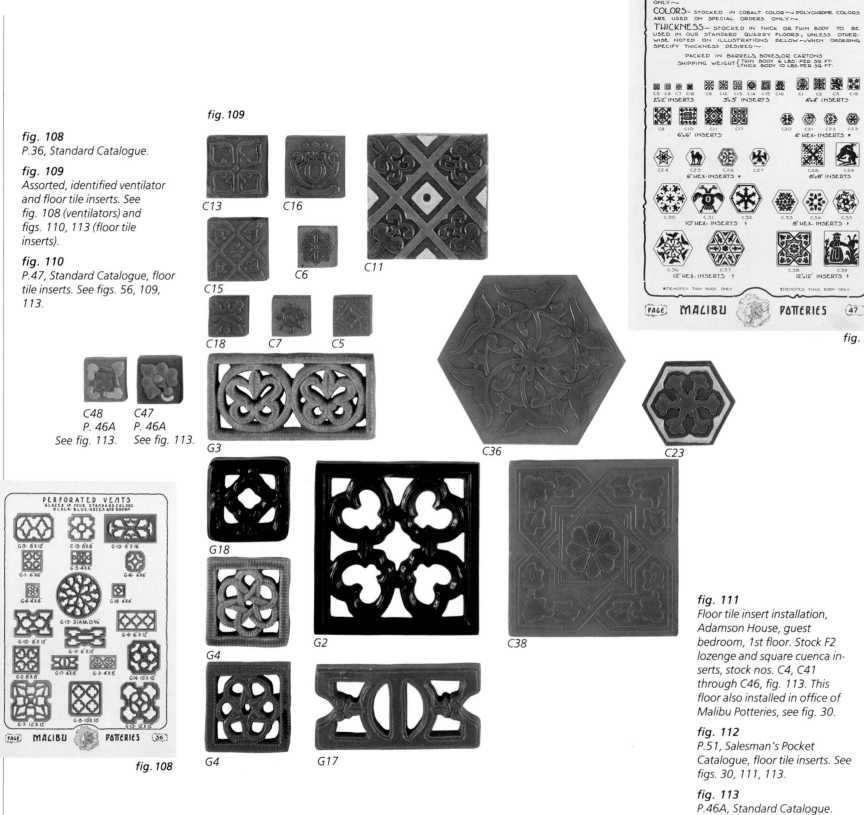

fig. 108
P.36, Standard Catalogue.

fig. 109
Assorted, identified ventilator and floor tile inserts. See fig. 108 (ventilators) and figs. 110, 113 (floor tile inserts).

fig. 110
P.47, Standard Catalogue, floor tile inserts. See figs. 56, 109, 113.

C48
P. 46A
See fig. 113.

C47
P. 46A
See fig. 113.

fig. 109

C13

C16

C11

C15

C6

C18

C7

C5

G3

C36

C23

G18

G4

G2

C38

G4

G17

fig. 108

FLOOR TILE INSERTS

DESCRIPTION— RED QUARRY TILE GLAZED IN DEPRESSIONS ONLY ~

COLORS— STOCKED IN COBALT COLOR ~ POLYCHROME COLORS ARE USED ON SPECIAL ORDERS ONLY ~

THICKNESS— STOCKED IN THICK OR THIN BODY TO BE USED IN OUR STANDARD QUARRY FLOORS, UNLESS OTHER-WISE NOTED ON ILLUSTRATIONS BELOW ~ WHEN ORDERING SPECIFY THICKNESS DESIRED ~

PACKED IN BARRELS, BOXES, OR CARTONS
SHIPPING WEIGHT {THIN BODY 6 LBS. PER SQ. FT. / THICK BODY 10 LBS. PER SQ. FT.

PAGE MALIBU POTTERIES 47

fig. 110

fig. 111
Floor tile insert installation, Adamson House, guest bedroom, 1st floor. Stock F2 lozenge and square cuenca inserts, stock nos. C4, C41 through C46, fig. 113. This floor also installed in office of Malibu Potteries, see fig. 30.

fig. 112
P.51, Salesman's Pocket Catalogue, floor tile inserts. See figs. 30, 111, 113.

fig. 113
P.46A, Standard Catalogue. See figs 30, 111, 112.

PERFORATED VENTS
GLAZED IN FOUR STANDARD COLORS
BLACK-BLUE-GREEN AND BROWN

PAGE MALIBU POTTERIES 36

fig. 111

fig. 112

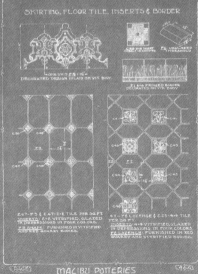

fig. 113

fig. 114

fig. 117

fig. 116

B143, P. 71 SPC, 6" x 6"

B145, P. 67 SPC, 6" x 8"

B147, P. 66 SPC, 6" x 12"

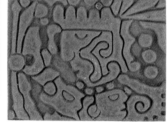

B144, P. 67 SPC, 6" x 8"

B157, P. 74 SPC, 6" x 8"

B146, P. 66 SPC, 6" x 12"

◄ fig. 115

fig. 118

fig. 114
P.66, Salesman's Pocket
Catalogue, Maya inserts.

fig. 115
Floor tile inserts, Adamson
House, east balcony. Square
cuenca inserts (yellow) are
stock nos. C1, C3, C19 (p.47
SC), fig. 110. Mayan tile inserts
are B105, B106 (p.64 SPC) and
B133, (p.65 SPC).

fig. 116
Assorted, identified Mayan tile.
Tiles B146 and B147 are illustrated in fig. 114. Tile B145
(p.67 SPC) is included in Mayan
fireplace mantel no. 26 (upper
left corner), fig. 118.

fig. 117
Mayan floor tile in entrance,
Mayan Theater, Los Angeles,
showing incised ornamentation.
See figs. 32, 33.

fig. 118
P.21 Standard Catalogue:
mantels made in Maya color
only.

fig. 120

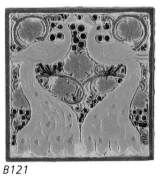
B121

B125

B59

fig. 119

B103-L

fig. 119
Assorted, identified mantel inserts. See fig. 121.

fig. 120
Dining room entry floor, Serra Retreat. Includes B115 (fig. 121). See figs. 37, 131.

fig. 121
P.17, Standard Catalogue, mantel inserts. See figs. 119, 122, 207, 208, 209.

fig. 122
Pattern of mottled mantel tile with mantel insert B119. See fig. 121.

69

B89

B124

B102-R

B123

B60

MANTEL INSERTS
MADE IN MATT POLYCHROME COLORS

PAGE   MALIBU   POTTERIES   17

fig. 121

B122

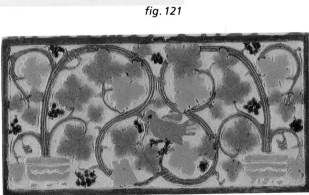
B84

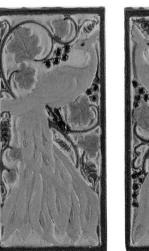
B118-L

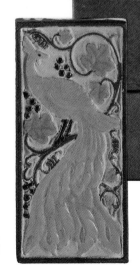
B118-R

fig. 122

A60

fig. 124

A58

A60

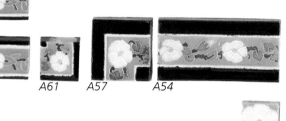

A61   A60   A61   A57   A54

fig. 125

N1

A43   A60

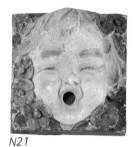 

A43   A60

N21   N21

70

fig. 123
P.11, Standard Catalogue,
bathroom tile trim. See
figs. 219, 124.

fig. 124
Assorted, identified bathroom
tile. See figs. 123, 219.

fig. 125
Assorted, identified fountain
spouts. See fig. 126.

fig. 126
P.50, Standard Catalogue,
fountain tile. See fig. 125.

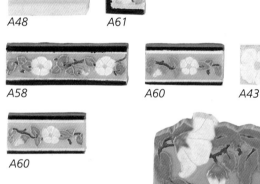

A48   A61

A58   A60   A43

A60

A51

A53

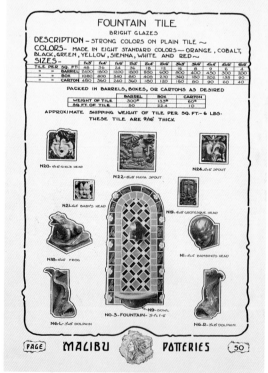

fig. 123

fig. 126

fig. 127

fig. 128

fig. 127
Neptune fountain, Adamson House, service corridor. Facing tile is design D-2 (E714). See fig. 128. Top border tiles are E721, E722, E723.

fig. 128
P.52, Salesman's Pocket Catalogue, Espanol tile. Tile D-2 (E714) is facing tile on Neptune fountain, fig. 127.

fig. 129
2½" x 2½" floor tile insert —
not in catalogues.

fig. 130
Assorted Malibu tile not found
in catalogues, assumed to be
special order tile.

fig. 129

fig. 130

fig. 132

fig. 131

fig. 131
Dining room entry floor, Serra Retreat, showing incised ornamentation in cuenca technique. See figs. 37, 120.

fig. 132
High-relief frieze panel, Malibu residence. Overall size: 3'6" wide, 8' high; red clay body, 137 pieces.

74

fig. 133

fig. 134

fig. 133
*Peacock Saracen panel with
finial top, 1'6" x 3', cuerda
seca technique. E24-P, black
background. See figs. 134,
139.*

fig. 134
*Peacock Saracen panel (same
as fig. 133), Malibu residence.
Installed with Saracen border
tiles E65 and E66.*

fig. 135
*"Poster Ship," Saracen panel
without border, cuerda seca
technique, E599-P. See fig.
139.*

fig. 136
*Saracen "Crow" panel, cuerda
seca technique, E597-P.*

fig. 137
*Peacock panel, Serra Retreat.
Cuerda seca technique, 3' x 3'.
This is the lower half of 3' x 6'
Saracen panel E621-P.*

fig. 138
*Urn and floral panel, 1' x 1'4",
cuerda seca technique, E585-P.
See fig. 139.*

fig. 139
*P.39 Standard Catalogue,
Saracen panels (murals). See
figs. 82 (E22-P), 83 (E23-P).*

fig. 140
*32-tile peacock Saracen panel,
cuerda seca technique, E631-P.
Nurse's bathroom, Adamson
House, 2nd floor.*

fig. 135

fig. 136

fig. 137

fig. 138

fig. 140

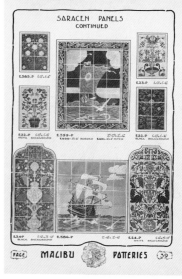

fig. 139

fig. 141

fig. 141
''Heraldic'' 12" x 12" floor
inserts installed in Friars lounge,
Mission Santa Barbara — not
listed in catalogues.

fig. 142
''Tea tiles.'' See fig. 12.

fig. 142

fig. 143

fig. 143
Cuerda seca table top, 30"
diameter, on Moorish floor
pattern using Saracen inserts E68
and E75. Living room, Adamson
House. See also fig. 190.

fig. 144
Smoker's stand, Spanish-design
circular buff bisque top, 10½"
diameter, cuerda seca technique.
See figs. 145, 146.

fig. 145
P.15, Salesman's Pocket
Catalogue, console top.

fig. 146
Smoker's stand designed by
J. Donald Prouty.
24" high with 10" diameter top;
4" diameter, 4 position ash tray
with 3-color drip glazes. Initial
production run was 25 units. See
figs. 144, 145.

fig. 146

fig. 144

CONSOLE TOP 15
K.7 10" DIAM.
K.6 ASH TRAY 4" DIAM
MALIBU POTTERIES

fig. 145

fig. 147
*36" diameter cuerda seca
"griffin" table top, Serra
Retreat. See fig. 150.*

fig. 148
*Small tile table-top with center
4-tile circle same as in fig. 147.*

fig. 149
*Decorative faience plate, 14½"
diameter, cuerda seca
technique.*

fig. 148

fig. 149

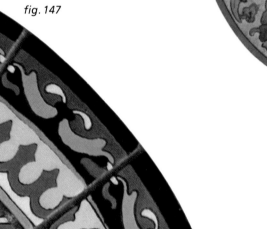

fig. 147

fig. 150

fig. 151

fig. 152

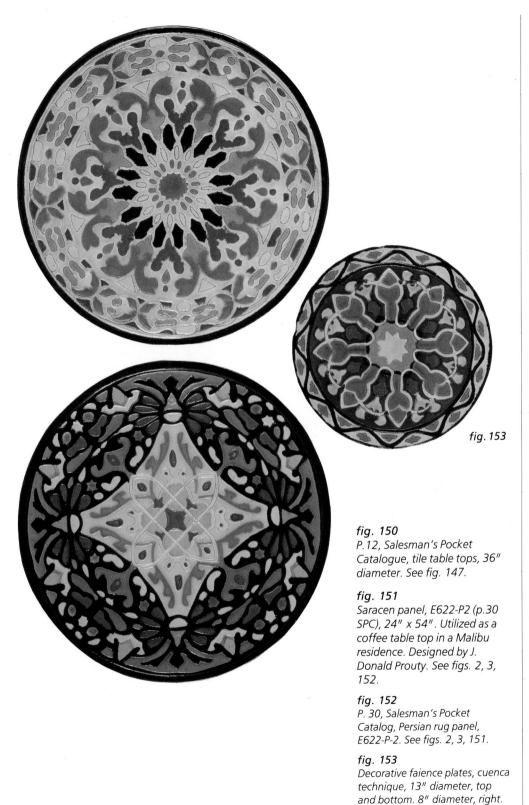

fig. 153

fig. 150
P.12, Salesman's Pocket Catalogue, tile table tops, 36" diameter. See fig. 147.

fig. 151
Saracen panel, E622-P2 (p.30 SPC), 24" x 54". Utilized as a coffee table top in a Malibu residence. Designed by J. Donald Prouty. See figs. 2, 3, 152.

fig. 152
P. 30, Salesman's Pocket Catalog, Persian rug panel, E622-P-2. See figs. 2, 3, 151.

fig. 153
Decorative faience plates, cuenca technique, 13" diameter, top and bottom. 8" diameter, right. See fig. 23.

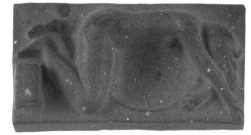

fig. 154

fig. 155

fig. 154
*"Reclining nude" pipe-holder,
3¼" x 6½".*

fig. 155
*Pair of elephant figures, solid
clay, buff bisque with gun-
metal gray glaze, 5¾" high, 3"
wide, 7½" long. Hand-pressed
in mold with many sections and
hand finished. Ears mounted
and tail attached after casting
(one tail goes right, the other
left). Glaze scraped from tusks
before glost firing leaving them
bare bisque for natural
contrast.*

fig. 156
*Jardiniere, Adamson House
dining room, 20½" high, 6"
top diameter.*

fig. 156

fig. 157

fig. 158

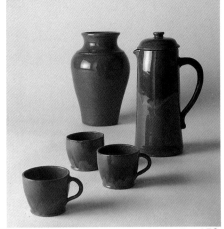

fig. 159

fig. 157
3 jardinieres, different glaze applications on the same shape, 6½" high, 5½" wide. Right to left: underglaze colors with clear, bright crackle overglaze; burnt sienna/red glaze; and cuerda seca colored glazes.

fig. 158
3 lamp bases: left. green glaze with jug handles; center. ivory and brown glaze with jug handles; right. rust and ivory drip glaze, traditional shape.

fig. 159
Blue and grey-green coffee pot with lid and 3 matching cups, inscribed "Malibu 1926," and green glazed vase.

fig. 160
Pair of "monk" sculpted bookends, 4½" wide, 5" deep, 5¾" high.

fig. 160

fig. 161

fig. 163

fig. 161
Pair of ship bookends, 4½" wide, 2½" deep, 5½" high.

fig. 162
Single balustrade column for Rindge mansion (Serra Retreat).

fig. 163
Two jardinieres, 18" high with 6½" top diameter, presented by R.B. Keeler to Mrs. Rindge. The left one uses the difficult red glaze successfully developed at The Potteries; the right is decorated in intricate underglaze colors with matt overglaze.

fig. 162

fig. 164

LOS ANGELES CITY HALL

O N JUNE 23, 1923, A BOND ISSUE, $5,000,000 for the building and $2,500,000 for the site, was authorized to construct a new Los Angeles City Hall. The building is distinguished by twenty-three decorative tile panels designed by J. Donald Prouty and produced by Malibu Potteries.

CHAPTER SIX

The site is bounded by Temple Street on the north, by Main Street on the east, by First Street on the south, and at the main entrance, by Spring Street on the west. The associated architects for the project, John C. Austin, John Parkinson, and Albert C. Martin, Sr., were commissioned to design the structure on August 17, 1925. The general contractor, C. J. Kubach Co., Inc., broke ground on March 4, 1926, the cornerstone was laid on June 22, 1927, and the new, completed Los Angeles City Hall was dedicated on April 26, 1928.

The architects were determined not to confine themselves to any particular style, which ruled out the Moorish-Spanish type architecture so prevalent in Southern California at the time. The book, *Los Angeles City Hall*, published in 1928 by the Los Angeles Board of Public Works, describes the architectural approach:

> *Grecian detail was adopted for the main entrance, while Romanesque was used in the arcades of the Forecourt, Rotunda, Council Chambers and the Board of Public Works Session Room. The tower and flanking wings may be regarded as "modern American," influenced, in a measure, by the present day set- back, or pyramided, type of construction.*[1]

fig. 165

This is the background to the challenge facing Rufus B. Keeler and J. Donald Prouty when Prouty reported to work at Malibu Potteries on the morning of July 1, 1927, just nine days after the City Hall cornerstone had been laid. Malibu Potteries was to design twenty-three decorative tile panels that would be appropriate for the architecture. Since traditional Moorish, Saracen, or Spanish designs currently being produced would certainly not do, entirely new concepts in design were required. Keeler assigned Don Prouty as the artist-designer for the City Hall project.

overleaf
fig. 164
Lunette and arched top panel at north and south stairwells, Los Angeles City Hall.
Lunette: 10' 10" wide, 5' 11" high.
Panel: 8' 4" wide, 16' 4" high.

fig. 166

fig. 165
*Los Angeles City Hall,
constructed in 1928.*

fig. 166
*Arched top panel, north
stairwell, 8′ 4″ wide, 16′ 4″
high. There are six of these
panels in City Hall: 2 each in the
north and south stairwells, and
on the west wall of the east
lobby.*

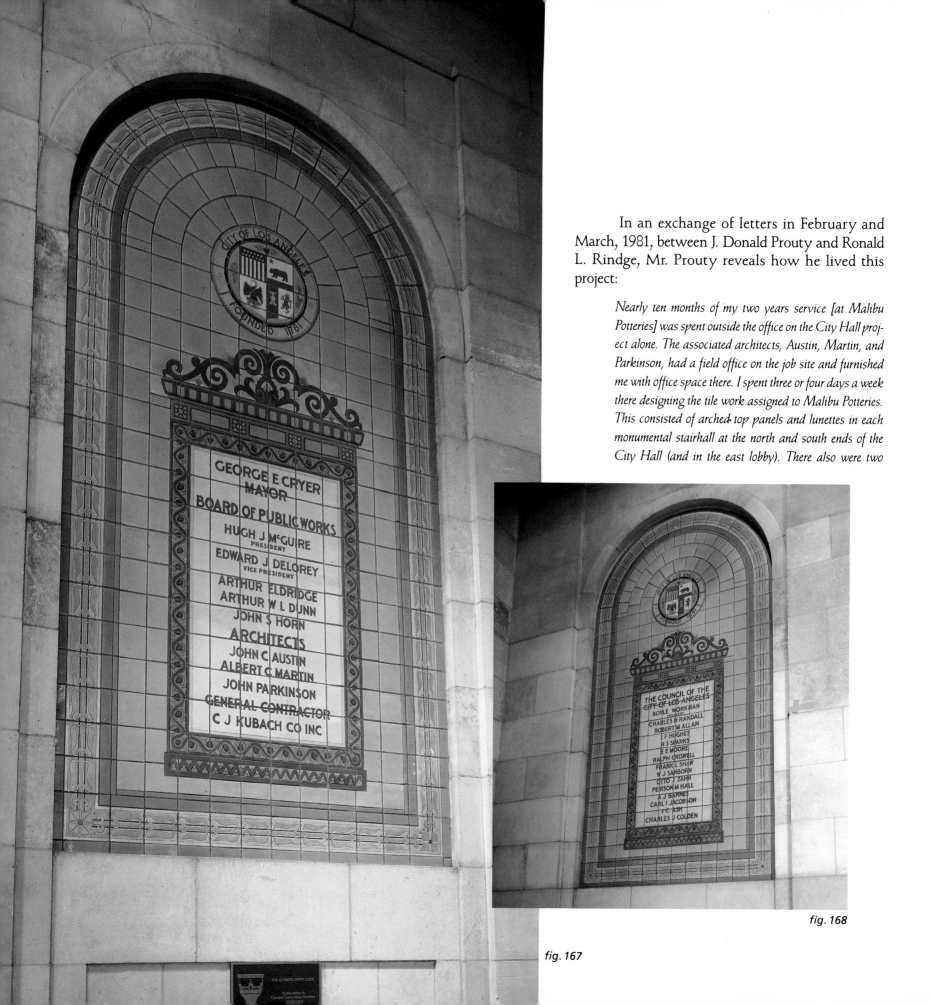

In an exchange of letters in February and March, 1981, between J. Donald Prouty and Ronald L. Rindge, Mr. Prouty reveals how he lived this project:

Nearly ten months of my two years service [at Malibu Potteries] was spent outside the office on the City Hall project alone. The associated architects, Austin, Martin, and Parkinson, had a field office on the job site and furnished me with office space there. I spent three or four days a week there designing the tile work assigned to Malibu Potteries. This consisted of arched top panels and lunettes in each monumental stairhall at the north and south ends of the City Hall (and in the east lobby). There also were two

fig. 168

fig. 167

dedicatory panels. . . in the narthex (entry vestibule) on the west side of the building, and another decorative panel in the City Council Chambers. Each panel had to be individually designed to exactly fit the recesses in the marble walls, furnished by other contractors.

The architectural style of the new City Hall was designated "Modern Classic" by its designer, Austin Whittlesey, which required an entirely new concept of ornamentation. None of the traditional styles of ornamental tiles would be acceptable. First the new style was developed by a series of preliminary studies for the architect's approval. Then several small tiles were made by hand to show how the finished product would look, when viewed close up and from a distance up to 35 feet. Next the architect's plans, marble shop drawings and masonry walls were measured for each of the panels to determine the size of the radial shaped units in the arched top of the panels. I then made outline drawings of each of the tile shapes other than standard rectangular so the factory could start producing the buff bisque needed for the project. These drawings were made to "shrinkage scale" (13" = 1'0").

Then one by one the panels were designed on color drawings at 3/4" = 1'0" scale as my "shop drawings," each of which had to have architect's approval. Then I made full-size line drawings of each individual ornamental tile which were blueprinted. One print of outlines only for the cuerda seca manganese and oil stencil, and a print hand-colored with opaque watercolor and glaze numbers marked in each area for use by the glazers. A bill of materials and a setting diagram was provided for each item. These production drawings were taken by me to the factory as they were completed so production could proceed on a controlled schedule. When design and production drawings were completed by me in the field office on the panel in progress, I then proceeded to design the next one.[2]

Mr. Prouty then describes his personal touch on the two dedicatory panels of glazed faience tile located in the entry vestibule off the main Spring Street entrance. One panel contains the names of the members of the City Council of Los Angeles in 1927, and the other panel lists the names of the mayor, the members of the Board of Public Works, the architects and the general contractor, all of whom were directly responsible for the erection of this monumental structure:

When the dedicatory panels for the narthex were being full-sized for all border and background tiles to be made by the factory, the architect was worried about the quality of the lettering and asked if I would do that part of it myself. Therefore, I made a full-size layout with spaces for joints, and placed lettering to avoid any chance of the interruption of the letters in every name by the joints. I took this to the factory, laid out bisque with 1/4" steel rod spacers for the joints, and traced lettering through carbon paper. Then with a small brush I outlined each letter with manganese and oil directly on the bisque. Factory workers then inlaid the glazes, brown for the lettering, cream for the background. The City Hall architect was delighted with the results.[3]

The City Council Chamber is described in the book, Los Angeles City Hall:

[It] is 104 feet long, fifty-four feet wide and thirty-four feet high, of the basilica type of architecture, with clerestory side aisles and a heavily beamed ceiling. . . The rostrum at the south end of the chamber consists of an arched canopy, supported by two monolithic, mahogany-colored marble columns of Rouge Acajou. Capping the canopy is a perforated and carved cresting of oak, with high lights emphasized in gold. The back of the rostrum is formed by a faience tile panel framed in marble. This panel is of conventional design in green shades and forms a focal point of interest when viewed from the opposite end of the room.[4]

fig. 167
Dedicatory panel, headed by the seal of the City of Los Angeles, 1928 Mayor George E, Cryer, Board of Public Works, architects Austin, Martin and Parkinson and general contractor, C.J. Kubach Co. Inc., in entry vestibule off Spring Street, 6' 8" wide, 12' 10" high.

fig. 168
Dedicatory panel, 1928 Council of the City of Los Angeles, Boyle Workman, President, and 14 other Council Members, in entry vestibule off Spring Street, 6' 8" wide, 12' 10" high.

Donald Prouty refers to this panel in his letter of February 14, 1981, when he wrote: "Another first for the industry was the use of matt glazes in subdued colors with the cuerda seca process for the decorative tiles in the panel for the City Council Chamber."

Mr. Prouty concludes his comments about his involvement with the City Hall project after his design work was finished:

> After completing all design work I left the City Hall field office and returned to the Malibu office on a full time schedule. Periodically I returned to City Hall to check the progress and solve problems that arose in setting the tiles. For that contingency a small percentage overrun was made of some decorative tiles. The unused surplus was boxed and turned over to the building manager for future emergency repairs. They may still exist.

Malibu Potteries did not provide all the decorative tile in the City Hall. In his letter of March 14, 1981, Mr. Prouty gives some guidelines on how to distinguish the decorative tile installed at City Hall by Malibu Potteries versus that provided by Gladding McBean Co. of Glendale:

> The eight tile panels (two sets of four) in the exterior arcade of the fore court leading from Spring Street were designed and made by Gladding McBean Co. of Glendale. This firm also did the other tile work found on the mezzanine and on the ceiling of the rotunda. I believe all the City Hall tile work was designed or furnished by Gladding McBean Co. and Malibu Potteries. All divisions of sub-contract work on the City Hall were split as equally as possible between two competitive firms to avoid any stigma of patronage.
>
> I offer the following which may be of use in identifying G. McB. tile work in comparison to Malibu's, particularly on the City Hall project or wherever found:

Malibu BISQUE: Light buff colored 5/8" to 3/4" thick

G. McB. Co. BISQUE: Tobacco brown with dark speckles, 3/8" to 1/2" thick

---

Malibu SIZE: Nominal 2" × 2"
 4" × 4"
 6" × 6"

G. McB. Co. SIZE: Seldom over 4" × 4"

Malibu JOINT: 1/4" joint allowed for and recommended for setting tiles

G. McB. Co. JOINT: 1/8" or less was generally used giving work the effect of mosaic.

Malibu GLAZES: Light colors: Cream, white, pale green, and light blue transparent or translucent came out clean and clear over the bisque. Other colors were rich and vibrant.

G. McB. Co. GLAZES: The light colors mentioned were shaded tans due to the dark bisque and speckles showing thru glazes. Other colors were muted and mottled.

Mr. Prouty describes the completed City Hall project and his subsequent endeavors with other architects to specify Malibu Potteries tile for buildings they were designing:

> The finished City Hall tile installation was widely acclaimed and photos were published in most of the architectural magazines. The architect of the City Hall had the interior decorator, who did the painted ceilings and walls, pick up the colors and design motifs in the tiles for his work. On completing the City Hall project, I worked full time in the factory studio except for the trips made to Los Angeles to the offices of architects to try to get Malibu Potteries tile specified and used in buildings they had on their drawing boards. This gave Malibu an edge over our com-

Location and Description of the 23 City Hall Panels

Entry vestibule-narthex:

1   Dedicatory panel-mayor, etc., fig. 167
1   Dedicatory panel-council, fig. 168

City Council Chamber:

1   Large panel, matt glaze, fig. 169

North and South Stairwell Entrances: (2 panels at each entrance)

4   Very large panels, fig. 172
4   Large panels, fig. 166
4   Lunettes, fig. 164

East Lobby:

4   Large panels, fig. 170
2   Large panels, fig. 166
2   Lunettes

---

23   Total panels by Malibu Potteries

fig. 169

fig. 169
Tile panel and surrounding architectural setting behind rostrum in City Council Chamber, executed in matt glazes, cuerda seca technique. 6' 8" wide, 14' 1" high.

fig. 172 ▶

fig. 170

petitors due to the fact that I was known to them as a fellow member of the Southern California Chapter of the American Institute of Architects (A.I.A.) and a director of the Los Angeles Architectural Club which had headquarters in the Architects Building.[5]

The City Hall panels attest to the excellence and wide-ranging capabilities of the people at Malibu Potteries. The rich and vibrant tile they produced is as brilliant today as it was when first installed in 1927-1928. In the spectacular setting created by architects, designers and craftsmen of an earlier era, today's Los Angeles television viewers often see Don Prouty's colorful panel behind the rostrum in Council Chambers during television coverage of the proceedings of the City Council.

The Malibu Lagoon Museum is grateful to the late J. Donald Prouty for providing present and future generations with insight on how this splendid tile work came to adorn the Los Angeles City Hall.

fig. 171

fig. 170
Arched top panel, one of four matching panels, east lobby. 8' 4" wide, 16' 4" high. See fig. 171 for detail of perimeter design. Two lunettes in the east lobby, 8' 4" wide, 4' 8" high, are not pictured in this book.

fig. 171
Detail of four-tile pattern found in perimeter design of panels located in the north and south stairwells (fig. 172) and in the east lobby. (fig. 170).

fig. 172
Arched top panel, 10' 10" wide, 17' 7" high. There are four of these very large panels: 2 each in the north and south stairwells. See fig. 171 for detail of perimeter design.

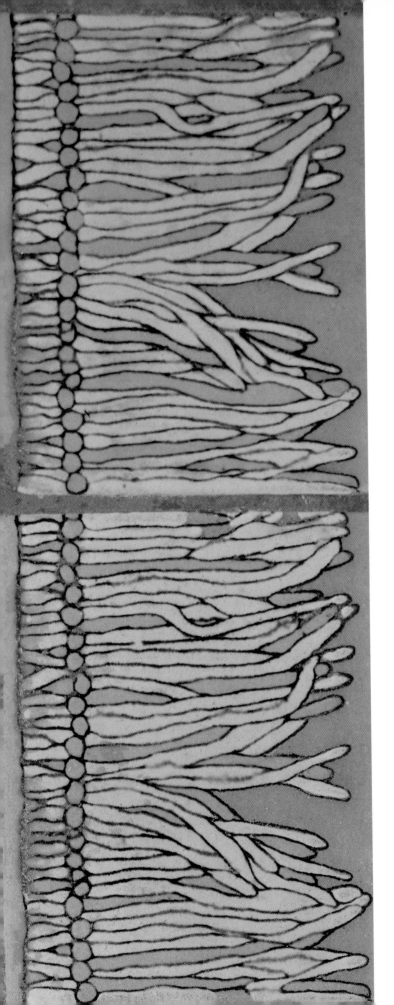

fig. 173

THE ADAMSON HOUSE

TODAY, THE MOST EXTENSIVE and impressive collection of Malibu Potteries ware can be seen at the Adamson House, located on thirteen graciously landscaped acres overlooking the world-famous Surfrider Beach and the "Malibu Movie Colony." This estate is a portion of Malibu Lagoon State Beach and is situated between the Malibu Pier, designated in 1985 as a Point of Historical Interest, and the Malibu Lagoon estuary.

fig. 176 ▶

overleaf
fig. 173
Detail of small Persian rug done in tile, cuerda seca technique, loggia. Fringe border tile is F1, fig. 113. William Handley designed the three rugs in the loggia. See also fig. 188.

fig. 174
Adamson House with star-shaped fish and lily pond in foreground.

fig. 174

fig. 175
Entry hall table, 2' x 4', forty-five tile cuerda seca technique. Inez Johnson von Hake (Chapter Four) created this intricate design.

fig. 176
Entry hall and stairhall to second floor. The custom designed stair-riser tiles are coordinated with 1' high decorative baseboard skirting, stock no. F4. See fig. 113. Note the handpainted wall cabinet doors repeat color scheme of the tile.

fig. 175

The Adamson Estate is also the location believed by many to be *Pueblo de las Canoas,* the site where Juan Rodriguez Cabrillo landed on October 10, 1542 and claimed the land in the name of the King of Spain.

This Spanish-Moorish Colonial Revival style home was built in 1929-1930 as a beach cottage for Merritt Huntley Adamson and Rhoda Agatha Rindge Adamson, daughter of Frederick and May Rindge (Chapter Two).

The Adamsons had three children: Rhoda-May, Sylvia Rindge, and Merritt Huntley, Jr. Merritt Adamson, a graduate of USC, was an experienced rancher and a lawyer and he and his wife, Rhoda, had established the Adohr Dairy (Adohr is Rhoda spelled backwards) in 1916.

Architectural Digest[1] in 1931 featured an article on the newly completed beach residence of Mr. and Mrs. Merritt Adamson. Construction was accomplished in 18 months under the expert direction of the talented and renowned pioneer architect, Stiles O. Clements.[2]

Working cohesively with John B. Holtzclaw, the interior decorator, and with Rufus B. Keeler, manager of the Malibu Potteries, Clements orchestrated an architectural masterpiece. Exquisitely handcrafted details – dramatic and graceful wrought-iron ornamentation, painted murals and intricate surface decoration,[3] vaulted ceilings – with the warm buff-colored walls for a background provided an ideal setting for the rich ceramic architectural accents custom designed by Malibu Potteries. There was lavish use of ceramic tile outside the home in fountains, a star-shaped fish and lily pond, murals, the bath house, etc. Some of the more elaborate installations were framed from inside the house by sensitively placed, elegantly detailed windows.

fig. 179

fig. 177

fig. 178

fig. 177
Detail of custom designed tile in girl's bathroom, second floor. Note the tile design motifs repeated in the handpainted door decorations.

fig. 178
Detail of custom designed tile in master bathroom, second floor. Border tile above window is E53.

fig. 179
Boy's bathroom, second floor has six ship tiles done in cuerda seca technique: E632P — 637P. Also includes E35, E574.

Large, colorfully glazed jardinieres with ever changing flower displays bedeck the courtyard walls leading to the front door, which is framed with bright floral ceramic panels. The tiled entry hall features an intricately patterned tile-top table, designed by Inez von Hake. A similar table top predominantly glazed in red, can be seen in the Malibu Lagoon Museum. A wide, richly hued wainscot, mounted flush with the buff plaster walls, frames the entry and complements the decorative risers as one continues up the vaulted stairway to a bright skylight-lit upper hall.

As well as its artistic attributes, this warm and livable home reflects the casually elegant lifestyle, the interests, needs, desires and dreams of the Adamson family. Fortunately, most of the original furnishings are placed just as they were when the family lived there.

The family's influence in the planning is suggested by examining books from their library and talking to family members.

Two beautifully illustrated volumes, *Majorcan Houses and Gardens* and *Provincial Houses in Spain*, include pictures of a ceramic dog bath much like the one in the service corridor – a practical yet decorative solution for a family who owned over twelve collie dogs, a Toggenberg goat, etc. A child's picture book of ships was used as inspiration for the crisply detailed ship murals designed by Donald Prouty for the son's bathroom. The Adamson family had a strong interest in boats and the water.

Each room portrays a different motif and color scheme reflecting the family's varied interests. The harmonious design is a testimony to the close alliance of the family, the architect, and the craftsmen, resulting in their inventive and creative architectural use of ceramic art.

fig. 180

fig. 181

97

fig. 182

fig. 180
''Venetian'' ship tile, upstairs
bathroom: E632P. See figs. 179,
181, 182.

fig. 181
''Viking'' ship tile, upstairs
bathroom: E633P. See figs. 179,
180, 182.

fig. 182
''Modern Liner'' ship tile, upstairs
bathroom: E637-P. See figs. 179,
180, 181.

◀ fig. 183

Harmony was frequently achieved in a room by repeating designs and colors from one texture to another, such as Belgian linen fabric, hand-painted doors, walls and ceilings, and custom designed ceramic products. The nurse's bedroom features a stylized road runner in the Belgian linen drapes, in the tiles under the mantel, and also hand-painted on the doors. Repetition of a floral motif in different media is also found in the girls' bathroom.

The striking floor tile border and baseboard in the dining room repeat the colors and are designed to coordinate with the vaulted, molded painted ceiling. Bold roosters border the living room floor.

A colorful ceramic clock face in an attractive ceramic setting is mounted above a tile-topped table, all blending with the Saracen-tiled kitchen. A cozy, colorfully tiled upstairs kitchen was not only a convenience for the nurse, but also provided a place for the girls to make candy and cookies without getting in the way of the cook downstairs.

fig. 183
Kitchen clock framed in floral, cuerda seca Saracen panel. Note sculpted ceramic flourishes at the left and right of the clock to soften the transition of the panel to the wall. 2' x 4' tile-top table below clock consists of alternating Saracen tiles, E704, E705.

fig. 184
Small bird detail in peacock fountain, east patio. See fig. 185.

fig. 185
Custom-designed peacock fountain, cuerda seca technique, east patio. Tile behind pedestal is E716. See fig. 184 for detail.

fig. 184

fig. 186

fig. 185

fig. 186
Upstairs kitchen, completely tiled including the ceiling. Floral pattern at left is comprised of E724 A, B, C, D.

fig. 187
Tiled dog bath, wainscot and tables, service corridor. Includes E535, E537, E539, E525, E527.

fig. 187

fig. 189 ▶

The ceramic bench on a tiled upstairs patio provides a resting place from which to view the decorative medallion over the door (executed by Margaret Curtis Smith), to observe the peacock fountain below with the star-shaped fish and lily pond beyond, and in the distance the tiled swimming pool, the Malibu Pier, and the foaming waves of Surfrider Beach.

The focal point of the house, as well as the most dramatic and impressive of the tile installations, is the 6′8″ by 20′4″ simulated Persian rug, complete with silk fringes, designed by William Handley. It is flanked by two smaller matching rugs extending the length of the elegantly decorated loggia.

Done in the cuerda seca techique, the red glazes used in the rugs were a recent development in the ceramics industry. Donald Prouty discusses the history of red glazes:

> Through the twenties no one had a red glaze that matured with other colors at 1900°F. The nearest thing to red at that time was a rose pink and a burnt sienna. When a red was required it had to be produced alone by painting the red areas and overglazing and refiring separately at a lower heat, (like the metallic luster glazes). In 1929 a British Ceramicist named Cecil Jones developed the first reds ranging from orange vermillion through oxblood that could be fired with other colors at 1900°F. He brought them to this country when he was hired as a Ceramicist by Claycraft in 1930. The entire U.S. Industry soon was using the new reds. Inez von Hake's Oriental rug tiles with their rich, brilliant reds could not have been produced before 1930. Existing tiles of unknown origin can be dated by examining the reds. Pre 1929 tiles with china overglazed reds can be distinguished from the later reds.[4]

Using the specially formulated glazes of R. B. Keeler and exacting, firing conditions, Malibu Potteries was able to produce this unique ceramic masterpiece. Other significant ceramic products at the

fig. 188
Simulated Persian rug executed in tile using the cuerda seca technique. Loggia, Adamson House, Malibu. 6′ 8″ x 20′ 4″. 674 tiles. Courtesy of the Craft and Folk Art Museum, Los Angeles: excerpted from the Malibu Tile Exhibition Catalog, copyright 1980. See fig. 173

fig. 189
Fireplace, guest bedroom, first floor. Custom designed urn and floral panel over mantel with matching, inverted triangular tile inserts around fireplace. Hearth is composed of tile fragments, a technique often used to provide a transition from one strong design to another. Vase on mantel is in fig. 157.

fig. 188

Adamson House include: unusual hearths constructed by placing tile end-on-end; floors downstairs of vitreous tile with colorful borders, inserts, or overall designs; decorative perforated ventilators. A stroll around the garden reveals other ceramic highlights such as several murals, a Neptune fountain, decorative tiled showers, changing rooms and bathrooms in the large bath house by the pool, walls framing the Moorish arched windows of the living room and dining room, and the walled area around the dog bath in the service corridor.

Though used initially as a beach cottage, the house became the Adamsons' principal residence in the late 1930's. Rhoda Rindge Adamson continued to live there after her husband's death.

Mrs. Adamson died in 1962. Exercising their right of eminent domain, the State of California carried out condemnation proceedings in 1968 and acquired the house and 13-acre estate. A year later concerned local citizens learned of plans to demolish the house to build a parking lot for Surfrider Beach. Spearheaded by Judge John Merrick and Ronald Rindge, the Malibu Historical Society was formed. They sought to have the house placed on the National Register of Historic Places. During the years that a decision was pending, the property was leased to Pepperdine University. Their chancellor, Dr. Norvel Young, used it as both a home and an office for 13 years. In 1977 National Register status was achieved. The State assumed operating responsibility for the care of the house and grounds in 1982 .

In 1985 the Adamson House was designated California Historical Landmark No. 966 by the California Historical Resources Commission, largely because of the lavish and extensive ceramic installations of rare and priceless tile from Malibu Potteries.

Letters written at that time attesting to the significance of the Adamson House included the following excerpts:

> All available evidence points to the fact that the extremely imaginative and extensive use of ceramic tile in the Adamson House is truly unique, making the home one-of-a-kind and a tribute to ceramic art in architecture.[5]
>
> It is significant—both as a major Spanish Colonial Revival residence designed by Mr. Clements. . .and as a show piece of the craft of architectural tile. . . Utilization of Malibu Tile. . .appearing as architectural accents. . .and in many creative manifestations indoors and out, the quasi-Oriental splendor and coloristic richness of the tile work is outstanding.[6]
>
> In my opinion it is as important an artifact of the twenties as the Gamble House in Pasadena is of the first decade of the century.[7]

Today, a volunteer organization, the Malibu Lagoon State Beach Interpretive Association (known as Malibu Lagoon Museum) works cooperatively with the State of California to provide interpretive information to the public.

The Adamson House garage has been converted to a museum with interpretive displays depicting the history of Malibu, including the Chumash Indians, the chain of title of one of California's richest land grants (the Rancho Topanga Malibu Sequit), the Rindge and Adamson family, the Rindge Railroad, opening of Roosevelt Highway, the Malibu Potteries, surfing, Malibu Movie Colony, and real estate.

As increasing numbers of visitors come to the Adamson House and view its impressive display of ceramic tile, the prophesy of Kathryn Smith, author of *Malibu Tile,* is being fulfilled: " It will certainly serve as the greatest surviving testimony to the artistry of the Malibu Potteries and as virtually a museum of its dazzling production."[8]

fig. 190
Living room floor. Striking Saracen rooster border (center) and complimentary colored cove base tile (upper right, E711) outline the perimeter of the living room. Tile placed end on end (upper left) provides an unusual hearth. Moorish floor pattern (lower portion of photo) contains Saracen tile inserts E68, E75. See also fig. 143.

◀ **fig. 190**

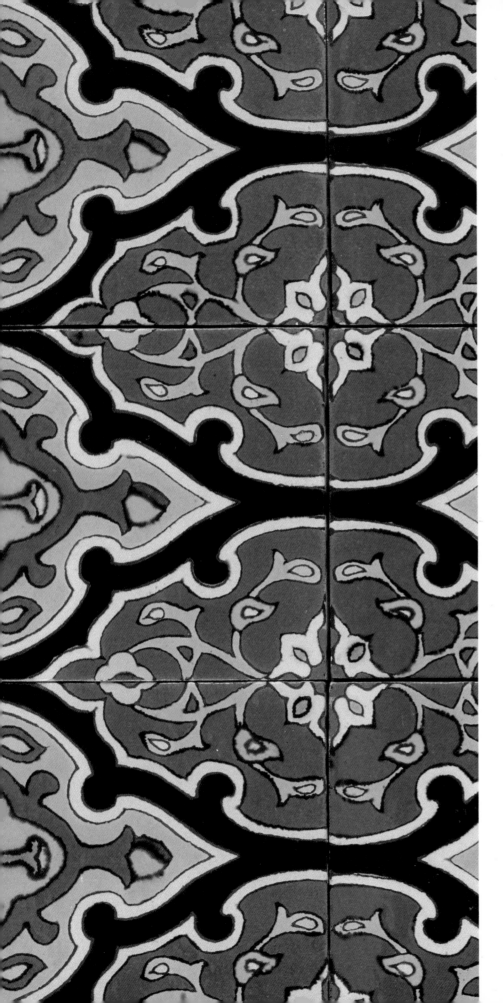

SERRA RETREAT

"YON BOUNDLESS OCEAN is the best symbol of eternity. As the blue sea receives its color from the sky above it, so can we receive the attributes of Heaven if we live under the obedience to God. The deep blue sea reflects the deeper blue of the heavens: so man's goodness reflects the greater goodness of God."⁴

fig. 191
fig. 192

fig. 195 ▶

overleaf
fig. 191
A statue of St. Francis, patron saint of the Order of Friars Minor, stands on an iris floral (fig. 205) tiled pedestal in the middle of a fountain adorned with E610 tile. See figs. 192, 199.

fig. 192
Eighteen-tile pattern, stock no. E610. See fig. 199.

These were the thoughts of Frederick Hastings Rindge in 1892 when he purchased the entire Rancho Malibu from Henry Workman Keller, son of Matthew Keller. He had realized his dream: "to find a farm near the ocean, and under the lee of the mountains; with a trout brook, wild trees, a lake, good soil and excellent climate, one not too hot in summer."[2]

In the lee of a hill much like he had described, he built a large Victorian ranch house in Malibu Can-yon. Frederick Rindge, a religious man, referred to this site as "Laudamus Hill," meaning in Latin, "We Praise!" The name "Laudamus" was indeed pro-phetic – for years later Serra Retreat, a many-roomed mansion owned by the Franciscans (Order of Friars Minor) stood on top of this hill surrounded by a valley on all sides and overlooking the picturesque Malibu Canyon.

Frederick Rindge died in 1905, and it was not

fig. 193
Rindge Castle on "Laudamus Hill," commanding a sweeping view of the Pacific Ocean and overlooking picturesque Malibu Canyon. Photo was taken before the fire of 1970.

fig. 194
Tiled decking and balustrade with tile inserts which survived the devastating 1970 fire. Includes C10, C17 (fig. 110); E19, E553, E704, E709. See also fig. 7.

fig. 195
Archway frames new memorial fountain created with salvaged 12″ x 12″ tiles from the Persian carpet destroyed in the 1970 fire. See figs. 80, 203, 206 and Inez Johnson von Hake, Chapter Four.

fig. 193

fig. 194

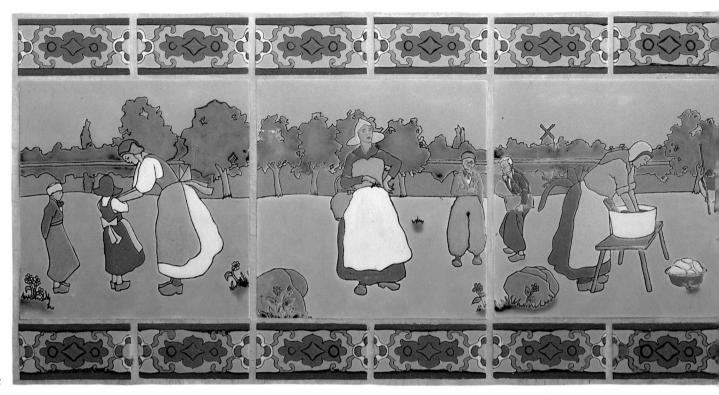

fig. 196

until 1929 that Mrs. Rindge was able to begin construction of the great house they had both planned for Laudamus Hill overlooking the sea. The prestigious architectural firm of Morgan, Walls and Clements, was retained by Mrs. Rindge. *"Residence for Mrs. M. K. Rindge, Rancho Malibu, California Job. No. 1617"* on the original blueprints was indeed an under-description of the 50-room authentic Mediterranean mansion envisioned by May Rindge. During the four-year construction period she poured over one-half million dollars into the castle-like structure featuring lavish use of marble, hand-carved mahogany and exquisite tile.

In addition to the practical business reasons for founding Malibu Potteries in 1926, it was said that Mrs. Rindge had an addiction to the beauties and the possibilities of tile. A high-priority project of the plant

was the custom-designed tile to be used widely throughout the "Castle" for floors, walls, and in some ceilings as well. For the huge baronial hall, the arched roof was to have an intricate pattern of mosaic tile, and the skilled artisans at the plant were also commissioned to produce in tile a 13′ × 59′ replica of a Persian carpet complete with simulated braided silk fringe.

Nearly a dozen rooms for the servants were tiled in varying styles and colors. The linen room, big enough for a luxury hotel, was done in blue and white tile. The sewing room had a blue and cream tile floor, with cedar closets lining the four walls.

In the huge laundry room not only the floors, walls and ceilings were finished in tile, but even the laundry tubs and the shelves were of tile. Around the

room was a wonderful panel in yellow and blue depicting Dutch housewives washing their clothing beside canals. Adjoining the completely tiled butler's pantry was the salad-mixing room, four times the size of the average housewife's kitchen, all in glazed tile. Next door the tiled canned goods pantry was complete with glazed tile shelves in soft blue, brown, yellow and cream. Except for its metal door, even the laundry chute was tiled.

In the suite built for son, Fred, Jr., the bathroom contained a 13′ × 17′ swimming pool. The big tank was lined with lead, but the tile was never set. The exterior wall of the library wing was embellished with the Rindge coat-of-arms in medallion form, worked in pastel shades of tile all encased in a Della Robbia-type wreath.

fig. 196
Six Dutch scene tiles adorning the walls of the laundry room. See fig. 197, and William Edward Handley, Chapter Four.

fig. 197
Former laundry room showing the extensive use of tile for floors, walls, and ceilings.

fig. 198
Original tiled bathroom, still extant. Includes E3, E38, E79, E95.

fig. 198

After the permanent closing of Malibu Potteries in 1932, the total inventory of tiles from the factory was moved to the unfinished mansion on the hill for safekeeping.

The "Castle" was never to reach completion, and the great structure stood on its hilltop as an unfulfilled dream. In 1936 it was taken over by a receiving company, and pursuant to Court Decree Mrs. Rindge was given a life estate in and to the great house, but sadly, she never occupied it. May K. Rindge died February 8, 1941, and the administration of the estate was in the hands of the Marblehead Land Company. It offered the property for sale, and in 1942 the unfinished mansion and its contents, together with 26 acres of land, were sold for $50,000 to the Franciscan Order to become "Serra Retreat House."

Franciscan Brother Benedict Schlickum, and Michael Braun, a tile setter, undertook the task of tiling the rest of the rooms. They found tiles were either stacked in the different rooms, or in crates and barrels with blue prints. The beautiful stairway tile was laid out and installed by Mr. Braun and Brother Benedict. They also found the tile carpet for the main gallery with its blueprint—all except 11 pieces, which were never located. These were made up finally many years later. Michael Braun remained at Serra Retreat for over twenty years, continuing to work with the tile as needed and acting as custodian of the tile inventory. After his death in 1966, the new Serra Retreat Chapel, decorated with Malibu tile, was dedicated in his memory.

Father Augustine Hobrecht, as Vice Provincial, took over the program for the Malibu hill. He felt the establishment would serve the Province best not as a seminary, as originally planned, but as a

◀ fig. 199

fig. 200

fig. 201

fig. 199
Circa 1943 photo at Serra Retreat shows group around the St. Francis fountain. Persons identified in photo are: 3rd from left, Michael Braun, who labored 23 years installing tile at Serra Retreat; 4th from left, seated, Fr. Augustine Hobrecht, O.F.M., Director of Serra Retreat from 1943 to 1948; and at the far right, Fr. Terence Cronin, O.F.M., Director of Serra Retreat from 1970 to 1980.

fig. 200
North wall, conference room. Tile table tops were used to produce the effect of stained glass windows. See fig. 202.

fig. 201
P.16 SPC, table top. See fig. 200.

fig. 202
42" diameter table-top, center panel of a hand-carved, Philippine mahogany "Reredos" (altar screen), north wall, conference room. This panel is flanked on the left and right by the two eliptical table tops shown in fig. 200.

fig. 202

fig. 203
Center portion of the 13' x 59' replica of the Persian carpet as it was laid out on the floor of the Malibu Potteries before installation. See figs. 80, 195, 206.

fig. 204
Malibu tile risers face a graceful flight of broad steps leading from the east garden to an upper bell-tower garden including the St. Francis fountain. In ascending order: E530, E543, E537, E532, E541, E543, E539, E528, E532, E536, E531, E535, E527.

fig. 205
Iris floral pattern installed on pedestal of St. Francis fountain, "Iris Wainscot" See fig. 191.

fig. 206
Companion planter for memorial fountain (background), also created with salvaged 12" x 12" tiles from the Persian carpet destroyed in the 1970 fire. See figs. 80, 195, 203.

112

fig. 203

fig. 205

fig. 204

fig. 206

retreat house. In spite of war-time difficulties and limitations, work went steadily ahead on that plan. In October, 1943, Father Augustine with Father Owen da Silva, opened "Serra Retreat." The gardens, by careful planning, had achieved an atmosphere of peace and quiet rare in this busy world. Softly the angelus bells summoned retreatants to prayer and holy song led by brown-robed, sandal-clad Franciscans. Week after week, Catholic laymen and their friends of all denominations and creeds, in quest of spiritual renewal came to meditate, to pray, and to hear God's voice in the quiet sanctuary of the Malibu hills.

Unfortunately, on September 25, 1970, the beautiful "Castle on Laudamus Hill" was destroyed by a horrifying brush fire that also destroyed many homes and buildings throughout the Malibu area. However, slowly and steadily the resourceful and dedicated Friars have been rebuilding. An administration wing containing offices, Friar's quarters and retreatant's rooms has been built over the mansion's original laundry and 9-car garage. And atop the original foundation of one wing also demolished by the fire, a beautiful dining room and modern kitchen have been erected. In both of these additions unmarred samples of Malibu tiles have been utilized in handsome table tops and in artistic wall hangings framed in oak. Other bits and pieces of salvaged tile can be seen imbedded in walks and wall insets throughout the grounds.

After the 1970 fire, only fragments of the Persian carpet were salvageable from the rubble. For ten years the 12″ × 12″ tiles lay stacked and unused, most of them encrusted with cement mortar, chipped or cracked. In December 1986, tile setters and brick layers designed and created a planter and memorial foun-

◀ fig. 207

tain out of the ornate tiles. Inez von Hake, who designed the original tile carpet in 1931, was invited to come and view this transformation of her artistry. As reported in the January 1987 newsletter of the Retreat House: "There were surely feelings akin to a mother's love as her hands lingered over these original works of her own, now in their second life, fifty-five years later."

The remaining original tile installations and the new use of salvaged tile are far from the ambitious tile display envisioned by May Rindge, the great lady who wanted them so much to enhance the regal splendor of every room in her dream "Castle" on the hill.

Nevertheless, they cannot fail to evoke in both the casual observer and the knowledgeable ceramist, an appreciation of the incredible artistic skills of the designers and fabricators who created these world famous Malibu tiles.

With that generosity characteristic of the Franciscans, appropriate selections of Malibu tile were given to the Friars at Santa Barbara Mission, Mission San Miguel near Paso Robles, and Saint Francis Retreat at San Juan Bautista.

These exquisite tiles can be seen today at Santa Barbara Mission installed in the fireplace and floor of the Friar's Lounge, the floor of the dining hall, risers on four different stairwells and in a garden fountain. At Mission San Miguel Malibu tile was used to face a beautiful fireplace in the Retreatant's Lounge and can also be found in a bright tile border strip in the library bathroom. Malibu tiles of a different design from the fireplaces at Santa Barbara and San Miguel were used for the unique fireplace at Saint Francis Retreat at San Juan Bautista.

It is fitting, indeed, that Malibu tiles journeyed the "Mission Trail" from Junipero Serra Retreat in Malibu to Santa Barbara, San Miguel, and San Juan Bautista where their ceramic splendor can be admired and enjoyed down through the years by the Franciscans, their retreatants, and thousands of history-minded Mission visitors.

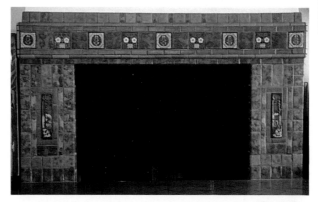

fig. 208

fig. 209

fig. 210

fig. 207
Fireplace mantel by Malibu Potteries, St. Francis Retreat, San Juan Bautista, CA. See figs. 121,210. Fireplace trim, see fig. 43. Hearth riser is E554.

fig. 208
Fireplace mantel detail by Malibu Potteries, Mission Santa Barbara. See fig. 121.

fig. 209
Fireplace mantel by Malibu Potteries, Mission San Miguel, See fig. 121, fireplace inserts. Depicted here: B102-L, B102-R, B124, B125.

fig. 210
Insert and mantel details on fireplace at St. Francis Retreat, San Juan Bautista. See fig. 207.

THE ONGOING SEARCH

EXAMPLES OF MALIBU POTTERIES Art Deco, Mayan, Moorish or Saracen tile can almost certainly be found in many residences and other buildings in Beverly Hills, Hollywood, Pasadena, Los Angeles, the San Fernando Valley, Santa Ana, Santa Monica, or other Southern California communities that were constructed between 1926 and 1932.

fig. 211

The Malibu Lagoon Museum hopes that information in this book will lead to the discovery of more examples of standard or custom Malibu tile installations in California or elsewhere, extant or not. It is also our hope that it will lead to contact with other former employees of Malibu Potteries, or their relatives or friends who can add to the personal histories that we already have. (See list of employees at the end of Chapter Four.)

In attempting to locate significant installations of Malibu tile, the authors discovered some noteworthy decorative ceramic tile which was not produced by Malibu Potteries. A delegation journeyed to Scotty's Castle in Death Valley for an extensive tour arranged by the Curator, Mr. James "Bow" O'Barr. After close inspection of the tile and discussions with National Park Service personnel, the authors are convinced that there is no Malibu tile at Scotty's Castle.

Another magnificent faience tile installation was discovered at a beach home in Santa Barbara County. Research revealed that Gladding McBean Co. was the contractor of record. However, all or some of this tile may have come from Malibu Potteries—possibly through a sub-contract with Gladding McBean. An historic photo of this ceramic art as well as pertinent technical information and specifications were provided by J. Donald Prouty who was at Malibu Potteries at the time this tile was being installed. Since there is no proof of a sub-contract, additional information is needed to resolve this mystery—ideally from old records of Gladding McBean, if they still exist.

Color photographs of possible Malibu tile installations or products should be mailed with accompanying detailed information (size of the tile, red or buff clay body, architect and date of construction if known, etc.) to Malibu Lagoon Museum, P.O. Box 291, Malibu, California 90265. Information about former employees should be mailed to the same address.

Since the Malibu Lagoon Museum is an all-volunteer association with no paid staff, we will respond to such new information as promptly as we can. If new information received over the next two or three years is substantial and meaningful, it is possible that a supplementary book about the people and products of Malibu Potteries might be published in the future.

The pictures which follow are believed to be Malibu Potteries tile installations at unknown locations. The captions are our only clues. If any reader can provide information on these particular photos, the Malibu Lagoon Museum would be interested in receiving it.

fig. 212

fig. 213

fig. 214

fig. 215

fig. 216

CONTEMPORARY
USES OF
MALIBU TILE

fig. 217, 218
Detail of mosaic design using pieces of Malibu Tile on exterior of office building, Santa Monica. See fig. 211.

fig. 217

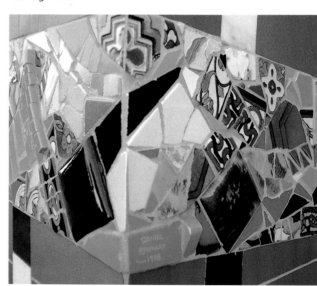

fig. 218

fig. 219

fig. 220

fig. 221

fig. 219
Coffee table, 1'6" x 3'8", 80 tiles: 24 gold pentagonal floor tile, 10 of E51, 38 of A60 and 8 of A43. See fig. 123.

fig. 220
Tile-top table, 1'4" x 3'10", 70 tiles. Includes 4 of E77, 4 of E515, 18 of E550 and 6 of E576.

fig. 221
Trivet utilizing 2" and 3" square tiles set in wooden frame with handles. Includes C18 (p. 47 SC, see fig. 110), E154, E167, E515. See also fig. 21.

NOTES

Title page

1. March, *Standards of Pottery Description,* p. 42.

Chapter One, CERAMICS, THE OLDEST OF THE CRAFTS

1. Manuscript, Keeler Collection, Malibu Lagoon Museum.

Chapter Two, HISTORY OF MALIBU POTTERIES

1. Rindge, *Happy Days in Southern California,* p. 64.
2. Prouty to Ronald Rindge, February 14, 1981.
3. Prouty to R. Rindge, March 4, 1981
4. Personal communication, Rorick to Toni Doyle, June 1987.
5. P. 122
6. Prouty to R. Rindge, February 14, 1981.
7. Personal communication, von Hake to T. Doyle, 1987.
8. Prouty to R. Rindge, March 4, 1981.
9. Sopp to John Rindge, September 3, 1973.
10. Prouty to R. Rindge, February 14, 1981.

Chapter Three, THE PLANT, DESIGN AND PRODUCTION

1. Personal communication, Dellamore to T. Doyle, September 30, 1986.
2. *Ibid.*
3. Prouty to R. Rindge, February 14, 1981.
4. Prouty to R. Rindge, March 4, 1981.
5. Prouty to R. Rindge, March 14, 1981.

Chapter Four, THE PEOPLE OF MALIBU POTTERIES

1. Personal communication, Smith to T. Doyle
2. Prouty to R. Rindge, February 14, 1981.
3. *Ibid.*
4. Prouty to R. Rindge, March 4, 1981.
5. *Ibid.*
6. Prouty to R. Rindge, February 14, 1981.
7. Prouty to R. Rindge, March 4, 1981.
8. Prouty to R. Rindge, February 14, 1981.
9. Prouty to R. Rindge, March 4, 1981.
10. Prouty to R. Rindge, February 14, 1981.

Chapter Six, LOS ANGELES CITY HALL

1. P. 14.
2. Prouty to R. Rindge, February 14, 1981.
3. *Ibid.*
4. P. 42 and p. 45.
5. Prouty to R. Rindge, February 14, 1981.

Chapter Seven, THE ADAMSON HOUSE

1. Vol. 7, no. 4.
2. Stiles O. Clements' residential work was relatively rare. His firm, Morgan, Walls & Clements, was usually commissioned to do large commercial structures such as the Richfield Building, the Pellissier Estate, Hollywood Turf Club, the Mayan, Wiltern, Leimert and Belasco Theaters – to mention a few.
3. Two Danish artists, Ejnar Hansen and Peter Nielsen, were responsible for painting and decorative murals and motifs in the house. Ejnar Hansen won over fifty prestigious awards for his paintings. His work is in the collection of the Los Angeles County Museum of Art.
4. Prouty to R. Rindge, March 14, 1981.
5. Richard Spriggs, President of the American Ceramics Society, April 5, 1985.
6. Ruthann Lehrer, Executive Director, Los Angeles Conservancy, April 18, 1985.
7. Dr. Robert Winter, Professor of History of Ideas. Occidental College, Apri 29, 1985.
8. P. 6.

Chapter Eight, SERRA RETREAT

1. Rindge, *Happy Days in Southern California,* p. 40.
2. Op. cit., p. 64.

BIBLIOGRAPHY

Architectural Terra Cotta: Standard Construction. National Terra Cotta Society, New York, 1914.

Austin, John C. "The Los Angeles City Hall." *The Architectural Forum.* July 1928, pp. 9-24.

Austin, Martin, Parkinson, Associated Architects. *Los Angeles City Hall – Acoustic Ceiling Tile & Decorative Tile. Job No. 270. Sheet No. 155.* (Blueprint). Revision 5-21-27.

Binns, Charles F., William H. Zimmer, Edward Orton, Jr. "Report of Committee on Equivalent Weights." *Manual of Ceramic Calculations.* American Ceramic Society.

Bleininger, Albert V. *The Collected Writings of Hermann August Seeger.* Vols. 1 & 2. Prepared from the records of the Royal Porcelain Factory at Berlin by Dr. H. Hecht and E. Cramer. The Chemical Publishing Company, Easton, Pennsylvania, 1902.

Brasfield, John C. (Publisher). "Los Angeles City Hall." *Architectural Digest.* March 1930, pp. 134-35.

– – –. "Los Angeles City Hall." *Architectural Digest.* March 1931, pp. 142-43.

– – –. "Adamson Residence." *Architectural Digest.* July 1931, pp.117-123, 178.

– – –. "Malibu Potteries." *Architectural Digest.* July 1931, p. 173.

Byne, Arthur, and Stapley, Mildred. *Spanish Architecture of the Sixteenth Century.* New York, 1917.

– – –. *Spanish Interiors and Furniture.* New York: William Helburn, Inc.: 1921.

– – –. *Provincial Houses in Spain.* New York, William Helburn, Inc.: 1925

– – –. *Majorcan Houses and Gardens.* New York. William Helburn, Inc.: 1928.

Ceramic Products Cyclopedia. Industrial Publications Inc., Chicago, 1915.

Dann, Frode N. *Ejnar Hansen. 50 Years of His Art.* Exhibition catalogue. Pasadena Art Museum, 1956.

Dietrich, Waldemar Fenn. *The Clay Resources and the Ceramic Industry of California – Bulletin No. 99.* San Francisco: California State Mining Bureau. January 1928, pp. 93, 106-107.

Dolmetsch, H. *Der Ornamentenschatz Ein Musterbuch Stilvoller Ornamente.* Stuttgart: Verlag Von Julius Hoffman, 1897.

Furnival, William J. *Leadless Decorative Tiles, Faience and Mosaic.* Stone, Staffordshire, England: W. J. Furnival, 1904.

Gebhard, David and Robert Winter. *Architecture in Los Angeles: A Compleat Guide.* Salt Lake City: Peregrine Smith Books, 1985.

Granjean, Rene. *Ceramique Orientale.* Paris, 1922.

Hales, George P. *Los Angeles City Hall.* Board of Public Works, City of Los Angeles, 1928

Keeler, Rufus B. "Silica and Alumina in Terra Cotta Glazes." *American Ceramic Society Transactions.* 1916.

– – –. "The Oldest of the Crafts." A paper presented to the   Twenty-first Annual Convention of the Tile and   Mantel Contractors' Association of America. Keeler Collection, Malibu Lagoon Museum.

– – –. "The Use of Clay Products in the Modern Home." *Bulletin of the American Ceramics Society.* July 1925. Vol. 4, No. 7. pp. 310-320.

– – –. "A Pottery Built on a Ranch." *Ceramic Industry.* May 1927.

– – –. "Dunting and Shivering of the Pacific Coast Clay." *The Journal of the American Ceramic Society.* December 1925.

Los Angeles Examiner. March 5, 1928. Two photos of tile work in the Los Angeles City Hall.

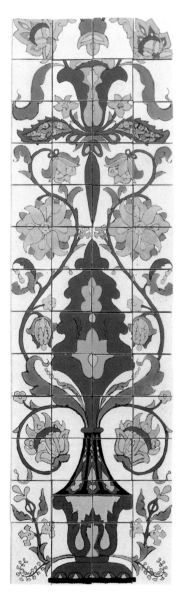

fig. 222
*52-tile Saracen Panel, 16" x 54",
cuerda seca technique. Tile marked "E60" but not listed in
catalogues. See also fig. 21.*

124

Los Angeles Record. "Epidemic of Bronze Vanity Hits
City Solons." September 6, 1928.

Malibu Lagoon Museum. "The Malibu Potteries."
The Malibu Story. 1985, pp. 31-34.

Malibu Potteries. *A Brief Outline of the History and
Development of the Malibu Potteries,* 1926

– – –. *Catalogue of Malibu Potteries,* 1926.

– – –. *Salesman's Pocket Catalogue,* 1926

March, Benjamin. *Standards of Pottery Description.*
Occasional contributions from the Museum of
Anthropology of the University of Michigan
No.3, February 10, 1934. University of Michigan
Press, Ann Arbor.

Meighan, Charles W. "The Use of Clay Products in
California Homes." *Pacific Coast Architect.*
April 1925. Vol. 27, No. 4.

Meyer, Franz Sales. *Handbook of Ornament.* New York:
Dover Pubications Inc.: 1957.

Newcomb, Rexford. *Architectural Monographs on Tiles and
Tilework.* Series. Associated Tile Manufacturers.
Beaver Falls, Pennsylvania:
No. 1 "Ceramics in Architecture," 1924
No. 2 "Ceramic Architecture in Ancient Egypt,
Babylonia and Assyria," 1924.
No. 3 "The Architectural Ceramics of Persia –
Ancient, Medieval and Modern," 1925.
No. 4 "Ceramic Art Among Greeks and
Romans," 1926
No. 5 "The Ceramics of Saracenic Syria, Turkey
and Egypt," 1926.
No. 6 "Ceramic Decoration in India," 1928
No. 7 "The Decorative Tiles of North Africa," 1929

– – –. "Color in Architecture." *Western Architect.*
January 1927.

– – –. *Mediterranean Domestic Architecture in the United
States.* J.H. Jansen, Cleveland, Ohio, 1928.

– – –. *Outlines of the History of Architecture.* Part 1 and 2.
Ann Arbor, Michigan, 1923-24.

– – –. *Spanish Colonial Architecture in the United States.*
New York, 1937.

Pacific Coast Ceramic News. "Serra Retreat at Malibu –
Unique Example in Tile," July 1955, p. 23.

Prouty, J. Donald. "Color in Italian Romanesque
Architecture." *The Technograph* 37 (January 1926).
University of Illinois College of Engineering.

– – –. "Decorative Tiles for California – An Ancient
Art Adapted to Modern Use Both Inside and
Outside the House." *California Home Owner.*
May 1928, p. 14-15, 20.

Rindge, Frederick Hastings. *Happy Days in Southern
California.* Cambridge, Mass.: Riverside Press, 1898.
Reprinted with biography added in 1972 and
1984.

Robinson, W.W., and Powell, Lawrence Clark. *The
Malibu.* Los Angeles: Ward Ritchie Press, 1958.

Serra Retreat. "The Serra Story," a brochure about the
Serra Retreat. Malibu, California, 1982.

Sexton, R.W. *Spanish Influences on American Architecture
and Decoration.* New York, 1926.

Smith, Kathryn. *Malibu Tile.* Preface by David
Greenberg. Los Angeles: Craft and Folk Art
Museum, 1980.

Southwest Builder and Contractor. "Public Gets Its First
Glimpse of Interior of Los Angeles Palatial City
Building." April 20, 1928, pp.35-39.

Speltz, Alexander. *Styles of Ornament.* Chicago: Regan
Publications, 1928.

Western Architect. Photos of Tile Panels, Los Angeles
City Hall. Plates 113 through 116. July 1928.

S T O C K   N U M B E R   I N D E X

This index lists in numeric sequence the Saracen and Moorish stock numbers (which were preceded by the letter "E") as printed in the Malibu Potteries Standard Catalogue. The index shows stock code, size, S or M for Saracen or Moorish, the page number in the Standard Catalogue followed by the figure number in parentheses if the page is reproduced herein, followed by other figure numbers which pertain to that particular stock code. "E" stock numbers not appearing in this book are not listed in the index. Other stock numbers appearing in this book are taken from either the Standard Catalogue or the Salesman's Pocket Catalogue (SPC). See page 3.

125

Stock no.	size / type		Stand. Cat. pg.	tile illustration (fig.#)
E91	4" x 6"	S	p.35	92
E92	2" x 2"	S	p.33 (fig. 104)	103
E93	2" x 2"	S	p.33 (fig. 104)	
E94	2" x 2"	S	p.33 (fig. 104)	
E95	2" x 2"	S	p.33 (fig. 104)	103, 198
E96	2" x 2"	S	p.33 (fig. 104)	37, 103
E97	2" x 2"	S	p.33 (fig. 104)	103
E98	2" x 2"	S	p.33 (fig. 104)	42, 103
E99	2" x 2"	S	p.33 (fig. 104)	37, 42, 103
E100	2" x 2"	S	p.33 (fig. 104)	42, 103
E101	6" x 6"	M	p.29 (fig. 88)	87, 89
E102	6" x 6"	M	p.29 (fig. 88)	16, 87
E103	6" x 6"	M	p.29 (fig. 88)	
E104	6" x 6"	M	p.29 (fig. 88)	87
E105	6" x 6"	M	p.29 (fig. 88)	
E106	6" x 6"	M	p.29 (fig. 88)	87
E107	6" x 6"	M	p.29 (fig. 88)	14
E108	2" x 4"	M	p.38	89
E109	6" x 6"	M	p.29 (fig. 88)	
E110	6" x 6"	M	p.29 (fig. 88)	
E111	6" x 6"	M	p.29 (fig. 88)	87
E112	6" x 6"	M	p.29 (fig. 88)	
E113	6" x 6"	M	p.29 (fig. 88)	
E114	6" x 6"	M	p.37 (fig. 90)	13, 61, 87
E115	5" x 8"	M	p.38	17, 89
E120	2" x 6"	M	p.38	89
E121	3" x 6"	M	p.38	89
E123	2" x 6"	M	p.38	15, 89
E125	4" x 4"	M	p.37 (fig. 90)	
E127	4" x 4"	M	p.37 (fig. 90)	89
E128	4" x 4"	M	p.37 (fig. 90)	13, 89
E130	4" x 4"	M	p.37 (fig. 90)	

Stock no.	size / type		Stand. Cat. pg.	tile illustration (fig. #)
E134	3" x 3"	M	p.38	89
E138	4" x 4"	M	p.37 (fig. 90)	
E141	4" x 4"	M	p.37 (fig. 90)	
E144	3" x 3"	M	p.32	89
E145	3" x 3"	M	p.32	89
E146	3" x 3"	M	p.32	89
E149	6" x 6"	M	p.37 (fig. 90)	
E150	3" x 3"	M	p.37 (fig. 90)	89
E154	3" x 3"	M	p.32	89, 221
E155	3" x 3"	M	p.32	89
E156	3" x 3"	M	p.32	89
E157	3" x 3"	M	p.32	89
E159	3" x 3"	M	p.38	89
E161	3" x 3"	M	p.32	89
E163	3" x 3"	M	p.38	89
E164	3" x 3"	M	p.38	89
E166	3" x 3"	M	p.38	89
E167	3" x 3"	M	p.32	89, 221
E169	3" x 3"	M	p.32	89
E501	2" x 2"	S	p.33 (fig. 104)	42, 103
E502	2" x 2"	S	p.33 (fig. 104)	42, 103
E503	2" x 2"	S	p.33 (fig. 104)	42, 103
E504	2" x 2"	S	p.33 (fig. 104)	103
E505	2" x 2"	S	p.33 (fig. 104)	103
E506	2" x 2"	S	p.33 (fig. 104)	103
E507	2" x 2"	S	p.33 (fig. 104)	103
E508	2" x 2"	S	p.33 (fig. 104)	

Stock no.	size / type		Stand. Cat. pg.	tile illustration (fig.#)
E509	2" x 2"	S	p.33 (fig. 104)	
E510	2" x 2"	S	p.33 (fig. 104)	
E511	2" x 2"	S	p.33 (fig. 104)	103
E512	2" x 2"	S	p.33 (fig. 104)	
E513	2" x 2"	S	p.33 (fig. 104)	
E514	2" x 2"	S	p.33 (fig. 104)	
E515	2" x 2"	S	p.33 (fig. 104)	102, 103, 220, 221
E516	2" x 4"	S	p.33 (fig. 104)	
E518	6" x 6"	S	p.27	92
E520	3" x 4"	S	p.34 (fig. 106)	
E521	3" x 3"	S	p.34 (fig. 106)	105
E522	3" x 3"	S	p.34 (fig. 106)	105
E523	3" x 3"	S	p.34 (fig. 106)	
E524	3" x 3"	S	p.34 (fig. 106)	
E525	5" x 5"	S	p.35	94, 187
E526	5" x 5"	S	p.35	93
E527	5" x 5"	S	p.35	94, 187, 204
E528	5" x 5"	S	p.35	92, 94, 204
E529	5" x 5"	S	p.35	93
E530	5" x 5"	S	p.31 (fig. 91)	94, 204
E531	5" x 5"	S	p.35	92, 204
E532	5" x 5"	S	p.31 (fig. 91)	21, 93, 94, 204
E533	5" x 5"	S	p.31 (fig. 91)	
E534	5" x 5"	S	p.31 (fig. 91)	93
E535	5" x 5"	S	p.31 (fig. 91)	20, 187, 204
E536	5" x 5"	S	p.31 (fig. 91)	93, 94, 95, 204
E537	5" x 5"	S	p.31 (fig. 91)	93, 94, 95, 187, 204
E538	5" x 5"	S	p.31 (fig. 91)	
E539	5" x 5"	S	p.31 (fig. 91)	93, 95, 187, 204
E541	5" x 5"	S	p.31 (fig. 91)	92, 204
E542	5" x 5"	S	p.35	25, 93
E543	5" x 5"	S	p.31 (fig. 91)	95, 204
E544	5" x 5"	S	p.31 (fig. 91)	
E545	2" x 6"	S	p.34 (fig. 106)	
E546	2" x 6"	S	p.34 (fig. 106)	105
E547	2" x 6"	S	p.34 (fig. 106)	
E548	2" x 6"	S	p.34 (fig. 106)	
E549	2" x 6"	S	p.34 (fig. 106)	105
E550	2" x 6"	S	p.34 (fig. 106)	105, 220
E551	2" x 6"	S	p.34 (fig. 106)	93, 105, 107
E552	2" x 6"	S	p.34 (fig. 106)	105, 107
E553	6" x 6"	S	p.37 (fig. 90)	194
E554	6" x 6"	S	p.35	49, 51, 98, 207
E556	2" x 4"	S	p.33 (fig. 104)	36, 37, 103
E557	2" x 4"	S	p.33 (fig. 104)	36, 103
E558	2" x 4"	S	p.33 (fig. 104)	36, 37, 103
E559	2" x 4"	S	p.33 (fig. 104)	36, 103
E560	3" x 6"	S	p.34 (fig. 106)	105
E561	3" x 6"	S	p.34 (fig. 106)	105
E562	4" x 4"	S	p.35	15, 92
E564	2" x 4"	S	p.33 (fig. 104)	103
E565	2" x 4"	S	p.33 (fig. 104)	36, 103
E566	2" x 4"	S	p.33 (fig. 104)	36, 103
E567	2" x 4"	S	p.33 (fig. 104)	103
E568	2" x 4"	S	p.33 (fig. 104)	103
E569	2" x 4"	S	p.33 (fig. 104)	
E570	2" x 4"	S	p.33 (fig. 104)	103
E571	2" x 4"	S	p.33 (fig. 104)	
E572	2" x 4"	S	p.33 (fig. 104)	
E573	2" x 4"	S	p.33 (fig. 104)	
E574	2" x 4"	S	p.33 (fig. 104)	179
E575	2" x 4"	S	p.33 (fig. 104)	103
E576	2" x 4"	S	p.33 (fig. 104)	103, 220
E577	2" x 4"	S	p.33 (fig. 104)	
E578	2" x 4"	S	p.33 (fig. 104)	8, 103
E579	2" x 4"	S	p.33 (fig. 104)	103
E580	2" x 4"	S	p.33 (fig. 104)	103
E581	2" x 4"	S	p.33 (fig. 104)	
E582	2" x 4"	S	p.33 (fig. 104)	93, 103
E584	4" x 6"	S	p.35	93

Stock no.	size / type		Stand. Cat. pg.	tile illustration (fig.#)
E585P	1' x 1'4"	S	p.39 (fig. 139)	138
E586P	2'6" x 2'6"	S	p.39 (fig. 139)	216
E587-miter	2" x 2"	S	p.35	92, 102, (see E557)
E588	6" x 6"	S	p.35	7
E589	6" x 6"	S	p.27	98
E592-miter	2" x 2"	S	p.35	102, (see E46)
E593-miter	2" x 2"	S	p.35	92, 102, (see E46)
E595	2" x 6"	S	p.34 (fig. 106)	
E596-miter	2" x 2"	S	p.35	93, (see E595)
E597P	1'6" x 2'	S	p.38	136
E599P	2' x 2'6"	S	p.39 (fig. 139)	135
E600-border	3" x 6"	S	p.39 (fig. 139)	(see E599)
E601-miter	4" x 4"	S	p.39 (fig. 139)	(see E599)
E610	6" x 6"	S	p.38B	21, 22, 191, 192, 199
E612	5" x 5"	S	p.38D	94, 95
E613	5" x 5"	S	p.38D	95
E621P	3' x 6'	S	p.38F	137
E622P	2' x 4'6"	S	p.38F	2, 3, 151, 152
E630P	2' x 1'6"	S	p.38F	74
E631P	2' x 4'"	S	p.38E	140
E632P	12" x 12"	S	p.38E	179, 180, (Venetian ship)
E633P	12" x 12"	S	p.38E	179, 181, (Viking Ship)
E634P	12" x 12"	S	p.38E	179, (Roman Galley)
E635P	12" x 12"	S	p.38E	179, (Santa Maria)
E636P	12" x 12"	S	p.38E	179, (Constitution)
E637P	12" x 12"	S	p.38E	179, 182, (Modern Liner)
E704	6" x 6"	S	p.38C	74, 183, 194
E705	6" x 6"	S	p.38C	74, 87, 183
E709	6" x 6"	S	p.38C	194

Stock no.	size / type		Stand. Cat. pg.	tile illustration (fig. #)
E711	6" x 6"	S	p.38A	190
E714	6" x 6"	S	p.38A	127, 128
E716	6" x 6"	S	p.38A	185
E721	3" x 3"	S	p.38A	127
E722	3" x 6"	S	p.38A	127
E723	3" x 3"	S	p.38A	127
E724 A-D	6" x 6"	S	p.38A	186
E737A-yellow	4" x 4"	S	p.38D	93

INDEX

boldface numbers indicate illustration figure #

PHOTOGRAPHIC CREDITS (fig. #)

Catherine Durlock 111, 186
Ed Foster 76, 78
Jane Hemenez 134
Rufus B. Keeler Archives,
Malibu Lagoon Museum
33, 38, 40, 41, 46-48, 53, 54,
212, 213, 215, 216
Charlotte Laubach 165
Fred May 132, 151
Malibu Lagoon Museum
26, 29, 68, 70-72, 75, 79-81,
174, 193, 203, 214
Mike McCombs, Modernage
2, 5, 22, 23, 25, 28, 31, 34, 44,
49, 50, 55, 56, 58-64, 69, 82-85,
89, 92, 93, 98, 103, 105, 109,
116, 119, 122, 124, 125, 129,
130, 133, 135, 136, 138, 144,
146, 149, 153, 154, 155, 158,
159, 161, 162, 171, 192, 219, 222
Nancy McFadden 73, 115

Marc Muench 1, 4, 7, 32, 37,
74, 94, 96, 97, 101, 117, 120, 131,
137, 140, 143, 147, 156, 164, 166,
167, 168, 170, 172, 173, 175, 176,
177, 178, 179-185, 187, 189-191,
194-198, 200, 202, 204-206
Andrea Page 8
John Rindge 39, 57, 148,
220, 221
Ron Rindge 87
Sue Rindge 141, 169, 207-210
Toby Schreiber 30
Serra Retreat 199
Robert Sinclair 77
Spence Air Photo Collection,
Dept. of Geography, UCLA 24
Tom Vinetz 188
Wende Wagner 12 bottom,
142, 211, 217, 218
Wayne Wilcox 27, 52, 65,
157, 160, 163